Panther Cha

Panther Chameleon Owners Guide.

The Captive Care of Panther Chameleons, including Biology, Behavior and Ecology.

by

Ben Team

ALL RIGHTS RESERVED. This book contains material protected under International and Federal Copyright Laws and Treaties.

Any unauthorized reprint or use of this material is strictly prohibited. No part of this book may be reproduced or transmitted in any form or by any means, electronic, mechanical or otherwise, including photocopying or recording, or by any information storage and retrieval system without express written permission from the author.

Copyrighted © 2016

Published by: IMB Publishing

Table of Contents

About the Author

Ben Team is an environmental educator and author with over 16 years of professional reptile-keeping experience.

Ben currently maintains www.FootstepsInTheForest.com, where he shares information, narration and observations of the natural world. When not writing about plants, animals and habitats, Ben enjoys spending time with his beautiful wife.

Foreword

Few animals are as odd and amazing as chameleons are.

Equipped with special skin cells that allow them to change color rapidly and tongues nearly as long as the animals themselves, chameleons are without equal in the animal kingdom.

Most of these adaptations have arisen in response to their arboreal lifestyle, as most chameleons spend their lives perching precariously, far above the forest floor. Fortunately, the lizards' feet are uniquely suited for gripping perches, and their tails are also ready to grip branches, should the need arise.

While this type of lifestyle may seem to make chameleons vulnerable to predators, Mother Nature has gifted them with laterally flattened bodies and a rocking gait, which allow them to disappear amid the leaf-blown leaves.

Their peculiar feeding technique allows them to snatch careless insects out of the air without giving away their position. They can even watch for predators as they eat, courtesy of their independently mobile eyes.

Who wouldn't want to spend time in the company of such amazing creatures?

***

While the world is full of remarkable animals, relatively few are well suited for captivity. Most can only be seen in zoos or on television programs.

But chameleons are different – with sufficient dedication and effort, most people can learn to care for a chameleon of their very own. In fact, keepers have amply demonstrated that chameleons are not only capable of thriving in captivity, but they will reproduce under the proper circumstances.

Captive reproduction is beneficial for all parties. It gives enthusiasts, scientists and veterinarians a chance to learn more about the lifecycle of chameleons, and it helps to reduce the number of animals that are taken from the wild.

***

This should not suggest that chameleons are easy to maintain in captivity.

Chameleons require a great deal of care and maintenance, and they are not likely to survive periods of neglect. You must be dedicated to your pet's well-being and willing to take the steps necessary to provide your chameleon with a high quality of life.

This includes not only supplying the labor for your pet's day-to-day care, but also weathering the financial burdens that accompany lizard ownership. To have a good chance at success, you must address these issues during the planning phase to avoid unnecessary challenges later in the process.

Purchasing a chameleon impulsively almost guarantees failure.

***

Of course, not all chameleons are created equally. Some are better suited for a life in captivity than others are. Proper selection is paramount to success.

The world is home to approximately 170 different species, and each one has its own unique suite of physical and behavioral traits, habitat preferences and geographic range.

Panther chameleons (*Furcifer pardalis*) are among the most spectacular of all the chameleons, and, luckily for those who wish to care for beautiful and interesting lizards, they are among the best suited for captivity.

As with any animal, the key to success is learning as much about the species as possible, as well as what techniques and approaches have worked well for other keepers.

While keepers have yet to devise anything as concrete as a "formula" for success, their prior successes and failures have illuminated a general path that leads to success.

This is not to suggest that all keepers follow the same path, as disagreements abound. An array of choices lie before you, with proponents on both sides.

In each case, you will need to weigh the various factors and make the best possible decision on behalf of your pet.

PART I: THE PANTHER CHAMELEON

Properly caring for any animal requires an understanding of the species and its place in the natural world. This includes digesting subjects as disparate as anatomy and ecology, diet and geography, and reproduction and physiology.

It is only by learning what your pet is, how it lives, what it does that you can achieve the primary goal of animal husbandry: Providing your pet with the highest quality of life possible.

Chapter 1: Panther Chameleon Description and Anatomy

Given their strange and unique body plans, chameleons are instantly identifiable creatures. However, the various species exhibit a number of morphological differences, which allow them to be distinguished from one another.

In general, panther chameleons (*Furcifer pardalis*) are one of the largest and most colorful species. With practice, their size, facial ridges and color pattern make it relatively easy to distinguish panther chameleons from other species.

Size

Adult male panther chameleons reach much larger sizes than females do. Males typically reach between 12 and 18 inches (30 to 45 centimeters) in length, including the outstretched tail. Males usually weigh about 5 to 8 ounces (140 to 225 grams).

Females, on the other hand, reach only about 10 to 14 inches (25 to 35 centimeters) in length and between 2 and 4 ounces (55 to 110 grams) in weight.

Hatchling panther chameleons are tiny, measuring up to about 1.5 inches in length (4 centimeters) and weighing less than one gram when they emerge from their eggs.

Color and Pattern

Panther chameleons exhibit a striking diversity of color patterns. Their colors not only vary with age and sex, but also with mood, health, stress level and reproductive cycle.

Obviously, as chameleons are capable of complex (and rapid) color changes, descriptions of their color and pattern are obviously subject to change from one moment to the next. Nevertheless, a few generalizations can be made, and panther chameleons typically change colors in one of several stereotypical ways.

All panther chameleons, no matter the sex or age, share a similar basic color pattern. Most individuals display a horizontal line that begins near the front shoulder and extends posteriorly to the vicinity of the rear hips. However, this line may be less distinct on some females (particularly those who are receptive to mating or gravid) and juveniles than it is on the mature males.

The line usually breaks up into a series of "dashes" near the posterior end of the line. This line is generally a light color, most commonly white, except in the case of gravid females, which often display a pink or salmon horizontal line.

Panther chameleons also possess a number of vertical bars that originate at the top of the back, and travel down along the sides of the animal. These bars frequently take on complex shapes, resembling the letter "X" or "Y." These bars are usually darker in color than the base color of the lizards.

Hatchlings
Hatchlings are rather drably colored, primarily clad in browns and grays. They may have hints of pink, peach or salmon tones, and they often display a light-colored lateral line.

As they develop, panther chameleons develop more contrast, with both the vertical and horizontal pattern elements becoming more prominent with age. Both sexes look very similar until about three to six months of age, when the males begin to gain substantial color and contrast.

Females

Female panther chameleons basically resemble hatchlings. They are normally clad in brown and gray tones, although they may display areas of white, pink, salmon, peach or orange at times.

When receptive to a male's advances, a female usually adopts a nearly uniform peach or pink coloration. Once gravid, females will display a strongly contrasting orange and black color combination, particularly when approached by a male.

Unlike males, who often vary in color from one location to the next, females tend to be similar looking, no matter which location from which they originate.

Males

Male panther chameleons are among the most spectacular looking lizards in the world. The exact color combinations displayed by males differ from one population to the next (as well as from one individual to the next), but most display the same general aesthetic.

Males typically display a green body coloration, with various patches of blue, red, orange, yellow and white. The horizontal pattern element is usually light colored, while the vertical bars are generally dark.

Males typically go about their day displaying a relatively subdued version of these colors. It is only when they become aroused – generally by noting the presence of another panther chameleon – that they "fire up" and display their boldest colors.

Some males may become nearly uniform blue, green, red or orange when thoroughly excited. In addition to the colors perceivable by humans, panther chameleons have been found to reflect ultraviolet light as well. (Witte, 2007)

Chameleon Skin and Color Change

Chameleons are infamous for their ability to change color quickly, but plenty of myths and misinformation surround this ability.

For example, although some species may change colors to avoid predators and blend with their surroundings (Devi Stuart-Fox, 2008), panther chameleons do not change colors for these reasons. Instead, panther chameleons – like most other chameleon species -- change their colors for social and thermal reasons.

As one would suspect of a species that changes color for social reasons, males have a much greater capacity for color change than females or juveniles do. Presumably, if color change played a large anti-predator role, it would be equally important for females, and perhaps, more important for juveniles.

Color change may indicate a change in mood, an attempt to intimidate rivals or (in the case of females) an effort to repel amorous males. They may also change their colors to raise or lower their body temperature.

Chameleons change colors with the help of their highly specialized skin. The manner in which their skin accomplishes this task differs from the way mollusks (such as octopi and cuttlefish) and some other creatures do so.

Chameleons have two separate layers of specialized cells (called iridophores) in their skin. Each iridophore contains a collection of small nanocrystals, which are arranged in a lattice-like configuration. By altering the arrangement of the crystals, they can selectively reflect different wavelengths of light. For example, by expanding the spaces between the crystals in the upper layer of iridophores, they can allow light to penetrate the lattice, making deep pigments visible. Conversely, they can tighten the lattice to reflect light and therefore suppress the visibility of the deeper colors. (Jérémie Teyssier, 2014)

The deeper layer of iridophores is thought to play an important role in body temperature and sun exposure. This layer contains fewer, but larger crystals, which are spaced more widely.

This lattice of iridophores reflects some of the infrared light striking the lizard's body, which provides some protection from the sun's strong rays when it is necessary to do so.

They may display amazing colors, but panther chameleons do not match their surroundings.

The Chameleon Head

Chameleons have relatively large heads, which connect to their bodies via indistinct necks. Unlike many other lizards, their heads have a relatively limited range of motion.

Panther chameleons possess a pair of ridges along the top edges of their heads. These ridges begin near the nostrils and extend along each side of the top of the head, continuing over the eyes and meeting at the back of the head.

Another ridge lies between the two ridges at the back of the head, which travels along the midline of the animal's head. A row of triangular scales lies along the midline of the gular region.

All of these cranial ridges are much more pronounced in mature males than they are in females and juveniles.

Eyes

Chameleons have some of the most incredible eyes of any animal in the world. The eyes are large and protrude from the head. Small scales cover the bulk of the eye and only a small opening allows light to penetrate the pupil.

Chameleon eyes are independently mobile. This allows them to scan the area for insects with one eye, while watching for predators or competitors with the other. When they are ready to extend their tongue to capture an insect, their eyes converge to facilitate effective targeting.

Chameleons have some of the most efficient lenses in the animal kingdom, and they are capable of magnifying images on the retina more than any other vertebrate lenses (once adjusted for body size). When targeting a prey item, chameleons focus through a technique known as accommodation, which means that they slightly alter the shape of their lenses to bring the item into focus. (Schaeffel, 1995)

Ears

Chameleons do not hear well. They appear to hear some airborne sounds, but sound is not a terribly important sensory pathway for panther chameleons. However, they can also feel vibrations conducted through the substrate (usually a perch).

Chameleons have no external ears, tympanic membranes, or middle ears, and their inner ears are poorly developed. Airborne sounds are detected by a structure called the pterygoid plate, just as they are in snakes.

While specific studies of panther chameleons are lacking, studies of other chameleon species have demonstrated that they can perceive frequencies from 100 to 100,000 Hertz. The chameleons studied – *Chamaeleo quilensis* and *Chamaeleo senegalensis* --were most sensitive to frequencies between 200 and 600 Hertz. (Wever, 2005)

Nostrils

Panther chameleons have two nostrils, which are located near the front of the snout. Special glands inside their nostrils allow the chameleons to excrete excess salt.

Panther chameleons have a relatively poor sense of smell, and olfaction probably plays a relatively minor role in the lives of these visually oriented lizards.

Mouth and Teeth

Chameleons have large mouths that extend well past the eyes. The gums are lined with sharp, triangular teeth, which are weakly attached to the top surface of the jawbone (called acrodont dentition).

This dental arrangement differs from the pleurodont dentition of most other reptiles, in which the teeth attach to the medial surfaces of the jaws. In fact, the presence of acrodont dentition in agamids is one of the clues suggesting that they are related to chameleons.

Chameleons do not replace their teeth over the course of their lives. (Abigail S. Tucker a, 2014)

Chameleon Tongue

The chameleon tongue is one of their most noteworthy features. Indeed the chameleon's tongue is a formidable tool, which has affected the entire evolutionary history of the group.

Able to extend to a length roughly equal to the chameleon's body (and, in some species, nearly twice this far), the tongue is shot from the chameleon's mouth at a very rapid rate.

The tongue achieves these high speeds via a catapult-like mechanism. The tongue is hollow and tubular in shape, and it wraps around a conical bit of cartilage called the hyoid horn. A ring of muscles surrounds the horn, and, when the chameleon is ready to propel the tongue forward, it compresses these muscles.

This causes the tongue to shoot forward and contact the prey item. The fleshy tip of the tongue creates a strong suction once it contacts the prey, which allows the tongue to bring the insect back into the mouth.

Limbs and Feet

Chameleons have four strong limbs, each of which extends vertically from the body. This arrangement allows the lizards to move effectively while balancing on a thin perch.

Chameleons have unusual feet, which are highly specialized for their arboreal lifestyle. Like most other lizards, chameleons possess five toes on their feet; unlike most other lizards, the toes of each foot are fused into two groups.

The chameleon's two outer toes the three inner toes are fused on the front feet, while the rear feet feature the reverse arrangement. Scientists often refer to animals with this arrangement as zygodactylous or didactylous.

Vent

Chameleons have a small opening – called the vent – on their ventral surface, near the base of the tail. The vent leads directly to the cloaca, and serves as the final exit point for waste, urates and eggs.

When lizards defecate, release urates or copulate, the vent opens slightly. Males may evert their hemipenes during defecation, but this is not as common with chameleons as some other types of lizards.

Tail

Chameleons have long, prehensile tails. When at rest, the tail is often held in a coiled position, but they use their tails to grip branches in the manner of a fifth appendage.

Chameleons do not voluntarily jettison their tails, nor do they grow replacement tails if the original becomes damaged.

Internal Organs

Despite their unusual morphology, the internal anatomy of chameleons differs relatively little from that of other lizards or tetrapods in general.

Chameleons draw oxygen in through their nostrils; pipe it through the trachea and into the lungs. Here, blood exchanges carbon dioxide for oxygen, before it is pumped to the various body parts via the heart and blood vessels.

While the chameleon's heart features only three true chambers (two atria and a single ventricle), a septum keeps the ventricle divided at most times, allowing the heart to operate similarly to a four-chambered, mammalian heart. This means that in practice, chameleons keep their oxygenated and deoxygenated blood relatively separate in the heart.

Their digestive system is comprised of an esophagus, stomach, small intestine, large intestine and a terminal chamber called the cloaca. The stomach has some ability to stretch to accommodate food.

The liver resides near the center of the animal's torso, with the gall bladder sitting directly behind it. While the gall bladder stores bile, the liver provides a number of functions relating to digestion, metabolism and filtration. Kidneys, which lie almost directly behind the lungs, filter wastes from the lizard's bloodstream.

Chameleons control their bodies via their brain and nervous system. Their endocrine and exocrine glands work much as they do in other vertebrates.

Reproductive Organs

Like all squamates, male panther chameleons have paired reproductive organs, called hemipenes. When not in use, males keep their hemipenes inside the bases of their tails. When they attempt to mate with a female, they evert one of the hemipenes and insert it into the female's cloaca.

The paired nature of the male sex organs ensures that males can continue to breed if they suffer injury to one of the hemipenes. This paired arrangement also allows male chameleons to mate with females on either side of their body.

Females have paired ovaries, which produce ova (eggs), and they have paired oviducts, which store the eggs after they are released from the ovaries. The eggs are shelled and held inside the oviducts until it is time to deposit the eggs. At this time, the eggs are passed from the oviducts into the cloaca and out of the body via the vent.

Chapter 2: Panther Chameleon Biology and Behavior

Panther chameleons exhibit a number of biological and behavioral adaptations that allow them to survive in their natural habitats.

Shedding

Like other scaled reptiles, chameleons shed their old skin to reveal new, fresh skin underneath. Chameleons do not shed their skin in one piece, as most snakes do, instead, they tend to shed in several separate pieces over the course of a day or two.

Chameleons may consume their shed skin, but this is not as common a phenomenon as it is in some other lizards, such as geckos.

Metabolism and Digestion

Panther chameleons are ectothermic ("cold-blooded") animals, whose internal metabolism depends on the chameleon's body temperature. When chameleons are warm, their bodily functions proceed more rapidly; when chameleons are cold, their bodily functions proceed slowly.

This also means that chameleons digest more effectively at suitably warm temperatures than they do at suboptimal temperatures. Their appetites also vary with temperature, and if the temperatures drop below the preferred range, they may cease feeding entirely.

A chameleon's body temperature largely follows ambient air temperatures, but they also absorb and reflect radiant heat, such as that coming from the sun. The lizards try to keep their body temperature within the preferred range by employing behaviors that allow them adjust their temperature.

For example, chameleons bask to warm their temperature when they are too cool. This typically involves orienting their body so that they are perpendicular with the sun's rays. Some individuals may exhibit darker colors when basking to help absorb more infrared rays.

By contrast, when it is necessary to cool off, chameleons may move into the shade or gape their mouths to release excess heat.

Growth Rate and Lifespan

Most chameleons, including panther chameleons, grow relatively quickly and lead rapid, brief lives.

After completing their lengthy incubation, panther chameleons hatch and begin feeding within hours or days. They grow quickly, and most wild specimens probably reach maturity in about three to six months.

Most individuals, especially females, live only a single season. Wild individuals rarely live longer than two years. Captive specimens, on the other hand, who benefit from the absence of predators and essentially unlimited food, may live longer than this. While females never live very long lives (two years appears to be about the maximum lifespan for females), males may survive for 5 to 7 years in some cases.

Foraging Behavior

Panther chameleons typically move relatively little while seeking food, but they scan their surroundings almost constantly.

This female panther chameleon has just captured an insect.

Once they see a potential prey item, they focus both eyes on it and adjust their bodies, to move within the optimum range for their tongues.

When they are in good position, they extend their tongues with incredible speed, hopefully scoring a direct hit on the prey item. Helped in part by a particularly viscous saliva, the tongue creates a suction effect, which keeps the prey attached as the tongue retracts into the mouth. (Fabian Brau, 2015) Once the prey is in the mouth, the chameleon chews the item a few times and swallows it.

Diel and Seasonal Activity

As one may expect from such visually oriented creatures, panther chameleons are almost exclusively diurnal. They typically rise shortly after sunrise and retire shortly before sunset. Panther chameleons sleep on some of the same perches that they use during the daytime. They may perch in dense vegetation or on exposed branches.

Panther chameleons remain active throughout the year. Mating usually takes place during the rainy season, with the resulting young hatching at the onset of the following rainy season.

Defensive Strategies and Tactics

Panther chameleons are cryptic animals that blend well with their environment. When relaxed, panther chameleons primarily display earth tones, which helps them escape the attention of predators. Additionally, panther chameleons possess laterally flattened bodies, which feature unusual spikes and projections; these features disrupt their outlines, which further help to camouflage the lizards. Chameleons also employ a rocking gait when they move. This is thought to help the lizards to blend in with the vegetation as it blows in the breeze.

Reproduction

Male panther chameleons mate with several females throughout the breeding season. Females may mate with more than one male or they can retain the sperm from a single mating and deposit multiple clutches of eggs over the course of the breeding season.

Males defend this territory from other males and attempt to breed with females that pass through it. Anecdotal observations suggest that males may remain in the vicinity of females with which they have mated, to guard them from other males.

The adults provide no care for the hatchlings, and may even predate upon them.

Chapter 3: Classification and Taxonomy

Chameleons are a well-defined group of lizards, who all spring from a common ancestor, and panther chameleons are a well-defined species within this group. Known to science for quite some time, panther chameleons were one of the first species described within the group (Cuvier, 1829).

Nevertheless, recent scientific inquiry has revealed a few surprising insights into these creatures. It appears that there is more to panther chameleons than previously thought.

But before delving more deeply into the classification and taxonomy of panther chameleons, it is helpful to begin with a broader context.

Although the taxonomy of lizards is the subject of great debate, the Integrated Taxonomic Information System currently classifies all of the living chameleons in the family Chamaeleonidae.

The Chamaeleonidae contains two: The typical chameleons (subfamily Chamaeleoninae) and the dwarf chameleons (subfamily Brookesiinae).

Lizards in the subfamily Chamaeleoninae are classified in one of six different genera: *Bradypodion, Calumma, Chamaeleo, Kinyongia, Nadzikambia* and *Furcifer*. Panther chameleons are in this final genus.

The genus *Furcifer* contains 20 different species. These represent some of the closest living relatives of panther chameleons – including the angel's chameleon (*Furcifer angeli*), which is likely the closest relative of panther chameleons. (C. J. Raxworthy, 2002)

Panther chameleons also exhibit some variability within the species, as the animals (particularly the males) living in different parts of Madagascar often differ markedly. Individuals living on Nosy Be, for example, differ from those living a short distance away, in Ambanja.

While all panther chameleons are currently recognized as a single species with no described subspecies, these regional variants clearly have some genetic basis. In fact, recent research has demonstrated that this single species harbors several well-defined clades. It appears that there may be as many as 11 different genetic populations of panther chameleon.

Some of these related groups correspond with populations that differ visually, while others do not. (Djordje Grbic, 2015)

The future classification of panther chameleons is sure to change, but it remains to be seen how these changes will manifest.

Chapter 4: The Panther Chameleon's World

To maintain a panther chameleon successfully, you must understand the animal's native habitat and provide a reasonable facsimile of it.

Range

Panther chameleons are native to northern Madagascar. They are restricted to the lowland forests found around the island's northern tip, from the vicinity of Ankaramy Be on the northwestern side of the island to Tamatave on the northeastern side.

Panther chameleons are denizens of the coastal lowlands, although they occasionally venture to elevations of about 3000 feet (900 meters) above sea level.

Humans have introduced panther chameleons to the islands of Reunion and Mauritius. As of 2013, a handful of live individuals have been found living in south Florida. Whether these individuals represent isolated escapees or a breeding population remains to be seen. (Michael R. Rochford, 2013)

Climate

Northern Madagascar is warm and humid throughout the year. The southeastern trade winds play a large role in the area's climate.

Throughout the range of panther chameleons, the temperatures usually remain between about 60 degrees Fahrenheit (15 degrees Celsius) and 90 degrees Fahrenheit (32 degrees Celsius).

The average temperatures in Ambanja (along the west coast of Madagascar) vary from about 80 degrees Fahrenheit (26 degrees Celsius) in March to about 74 degrees Fahrenheit (23 degrees Celsius) in July.

Likewise, average temperatures in Tamatave (on the east coast of Madagascar) range from 68 degrees Fahrenheit (20 degrees Celsius) in July to about 78 degrees Fahrenheit (25 degrees Celsius) in February.

The basic precipitation pattern for the coastal areas of northern Madagascar features a rainy season that stretches from November through March and a dry season that lasts from about April to October.

However, this pattern varies slightly on each coast. While the eastern locales receive more annual rainfall, they experience a very dramatic difference between the wet and dry seasons, whereas the western locales do not dry out as much from May to November.

In eastern locales, such as Tamatave and Sambava, rainfall varies between about 4 inches (10 centimeters) per month in the dry season, to about 18 inches (45 centimeters) per month during the peak of the wet season.

Meanwhile, rainfall in west coast locales, such as Ambanja and Nosy Be, varies from less than 2 inches (5 centimeters) per month in the dry season to more than 18 inches (45 centimeters) per month in the wet season.

Habitat

Panther chameleons primarily inhabit lowland forests. More specifically, panther chameleons appear to be drawn to edge habitats, where the forest grows adjacent to other habitat types. (F. ANDREONE 1, 2005)

Historically, it appears that panther chameleons preferred living in trees alongside riparian areas and forest clearings. However, modern panther chameleons seem to be making the best of the increasingly disturbed nature of coastal habitats, and relying on forest bands that parallel roads and trails.

Indeed, collectors and scientists often find the highest densities in such places. Panther chameleons are also common near agricultural fields. (Rabearivony, Brady, Jenkins, & Ravoahangimalala, 2007)

By eschewing dense forests, panther chameleons are presumably better able to see other chameleons in the area. This allows males to maintain and defend territories more effectively than they would in closed-canopy regions. These open habitats may also provide additional basking opportunities for the lizards.

Ironically, this preference for disturbed habitats may allow the panther chameleon to better withstand the habitat alterations taking place in Madagascar than other chameleons will.

Status in the Wild

Panther chameleons are abundant in several locations throughout their range. However, habitat destruction and collection for the pet trade certainly take their toll on wild populations.

Nevertheless, as panther chameleons appear to thrive in many disturbed habitats, and they feature a rapid growth

31

rate and lifecycle, the IUCN Red List of Threatened Species classifies the lizards in the "Least Concern" category.

Nearly half a million individuals were estimated to be living on the island of Nosy Be in a 2005 study. (F. ANDREONE, 2005) Overall population densities in some locations are estimated to be about two lizards per hectare of suitable habitat. (J. CHRISTIAN RANDRIANANTOANDRO, 2009)

Natural Diet

Wild panther chameleons consume a variety of invertebrates and small vertebrates. While few studies have directly examined the diet of wild panther chameleons, they likely consume the following types of prey items:

- Lepidopterans (adult butterflies, moths, skippers and larvae)
- Coleopterans (adult beetles and larvae)
- Dipterans (adult flies, crane flies, mosquitoes and larvae)
- Orthopterans (grasshoppers, katydids and crickets)
- Mollusks (snails and slugs)
- Annelids (earthworms)
- Arachnids (spiders and harvestmen)
- Reptiles (small lizards)
- Amphibians (small frogs)
- Avians (small birds)

In addition to animal prey, panther chameleons also consume a small amount of vegetation in the wild. This normally takes the form of leaves, but they also eat flowers and fruit.

Natural Predators

Virtually every predator in their range, including birds, snakes, frogs, lizards, spiders and even other chameleons, hunt hatchling panther chameleons. Because the small lizards have few ways to protect themselves (aside from trying to remain out of sight), it is likely that a large percentage of the hatchlings from each clutch are eaten before they reach maturity.

There are some reports of panther chameleon hatchlings climbing up tall canopy trees, which is presumably a behavior that helps them avoid predators.

Things are not much better for mature chameleons. While adults needn't worry about spiders or other chameleons consuming them, several birds of prey and snakes predate upon chameleons of all sizes. (RICHARD K. B. JENKINS, 2009)

Some of the predators native to Madagascar that are known to prey on chameleons (including panther chameleons) include:

Birds

- Banded kestrel (*Falco zoniventris*)
- Madagascan serpent eagle (*Eutriorchis astur*)
- Madagascar buzzard (*Buteo brachypterus*)
- Hook-billed vanga (*Vanga curvirostris*)
- Short-legged ground roller (*Brachypteracias leptosomus*)
- Malagasy harrier (*Circus macrosceles*)
- Madagascar harrier-hawk (*Polyboroides radiates*)
- Helmeted vaga (*Euryceros prevostii*)
- Barn owl (*Tyto alba*)
- Bernier's vanga (*Oriolia bernieri*)

- Peregrine falcon (*Falco peregrinus*)
- Madagascar owl (*Asio madagascariensis*)
- Red owl (*Tyto soumagnei*)
- Madagascan fish eagle (*Haliaeetus vociferoides*)
- Scaly ground roller (*Geobiastes squamiger*)
- Malagasy kestrel (*Falco newtoni*)
- Frances's sparrow hawk (*Accipiter francesii*)
- Blue coua (*Coua caerulea*)
- Madagascar cuckoo-hawk (*Aviceda madagascariensis*)
- Cuckoo roller (*Leptosomus discolor*)
- White-browed hawk-owl (*Ninox superciliaris*)
- White-headed vaga (*Leptopterus viridis*)
- Pygmy kingfisher (*Corythornis madagascariensis*)
- Pitta-like ground roller (*Atelornis pittoides*)
- White-throated rail (*Dryolimnas cuvieri*)
- Rainforest scops owl (*Otus rutilus*)

Mammals

- Fossa (*Cryptoprocta ferox*)
- Ring-tailed lemur (*Lemur catta*)

Reptiles

- Pencil snake (*Mimophis mahafaliensis*)
- Malagasy cat-eyed snake (*Madagascarophis meriodionalis*)
- Malagasy tree snake (*Stenophis betsileanus*)
- Perinet night snake (*Ithycyphus perineti*)
- Southwestern night snake (*Ithycyphus oursi*)

Amphibians

- Fort Madagascar frog (*Mantidactylus femoralis*)
- Mascarene grass frog (*Ptychadena madagascariensis*)

PART II: PANTHER CHAMELEON HUSBANDRY

Once equipped with a basic understanding of what panther chameleons *are* (Chapter 1 and Chapter 3), where they *live* (Chapter 4), and what they *do* (Chapter 2) you can begin learning about their captive care.

Animal husbandry is an evolving pursuit. Keepers shift their strategies frequently as they incorporate new information and ideas into their husbandry paradigms.

There are few "right" or "wrong" answers, and what works in one situation may not work in another. Accordingly, you may find that different authorities present different, and sometimes conflicting, information regarding the care of these chameleons.

In all cases, you must strive to learn as much as you can about your pet and its natural habitat, so that you may provide it with the best quality of life possible.

Chapter 5: Panther Chameleons as Pets

Panther chameleons can make rewarding pets, but you must know what to expect before adding one to your home and family. This includes not only understanding the nature of the care they require, but also the costs associated with this care.

Assuming that you feel confident in your ability to care for a panther chameleon and endure the associated financial burdens, you can begin seeking your individual pet.

Understanding the Commitment

Keeping a panther chameleon as a pet requires a substantial commitment. You will be responsible for your pet's well-being for the rest of its life. Although panther chameleons are not particularly long-lived animals, their lifespans are not trivial.

Can you be sure that you will still want to care for your pet several years in the future? Do you know what your living situation will be? What changes will have occurred in your family? How will your working life have changed over this time?

You must consider all of these possibilities before acquiring a new pet. Failing to do so often leads to apathy, neglect and even resentment, which is not good for you or your pet lizard.

Neglecting your pet is wrong, and in some locations, a criminal offense. You must continue to provide quality care for your chameleon, even once the novelty has worn off, and it is no longer fun to clean the cage and purchase crickets a few times a week.

Once you purchase a chameleon, its well-being becomes your responsibility until it passes away at the end of a long life, or you have found someone who will agree to adopt the animal for you.

Unfortunately, this is rarely an easy task. You may begin with thoughts of selling your pet to help recoup a small part of your investment, but these efforts will largely fall flat.

While professional breeders may profit from the sale of panther chameleons, amateurs are at a decided disadvantage. Only a tiny sliver of the general population is interested in reptilian pets, and only a small subset of these are interested in keeping panther chameleons.

Of those who are interested in acquiring a panther chameleon, most would rather start fresh, by *purchasing* a small hatchling or juvenile from an established breeder, rather than adopting your questionable animal *for free.*

After having difficulty finding a willing party to purchase or adopt your animal, many owners try to donate their pet to a local zoo. Unfortunately, this rarely works either.

Zoos are not interested in your pet chameleon, no matter how pretty he is and how readily he snatches crickets from your fingers. He is a pet with little to no reliable provenance and questionable health status. This is simply not the type of animal zoos are eager to add to their multi-million dollar collections.

Zoos obtain most of their animals from other zoos and museums; failing that, they obtain their animals directly from their land of origin. As a rule, they do not accept donated pets.

No matter how difficult it becomes to find a new home for your unwanted chameleon, you must never release non-native reptiles into the wild.

Chameleons can colonize places outside their native range (and they already have do so in some places). While these exotic populations do not appear to be causing serious ecological problems yet, further research is necessary before the potential for serious ecological damage can be ruled out.

Additionally, released or escaped reptiles cause a great deal of distress to those who are frightened by them. This leads local municipalities to adopt pet restrictions or ban reptile keeping entirely.

While the chances of an escaped or released chameleon harming anyone are very low, it is unlikely that those who fear reptiles will see the threat as minor.

The Costs of Captivity

Reptiles are often marketed as low-cost pets. While true in a relative sense (the costs associated with dog, cat, horse or tropical fish husbandry are often much higher than they are for panther chameleons), potential keepers must still prepare for the financial implications of chameleon ownership.

At the outset, you must budget for the acquisition of your pet, as well as the costs of purchasing or constructing a habitat. Unfortunately, while many keepers plan for these costs, they typically fail to consider the on-going costs, which will quickly eclipse the initial startup costs.

Startup Costs

One surprising fact most new keepers learn is the enclosure and equipment will often cost more than the animal does (except in the case of very high-priced specimens).

Prices fluctuate from one market to the next, but in general, the least you will spend on a male (females are often slightly less expensive) panther chameleon is about $200 (£135), while the least you will spend on the *initial* habitat and assorted equipment will be about $250 (£170). Replacement equipment and food will represent additional (and ongoing) expenses.

Examine the charts on the following pages to get an idea of three different pricing scenarios. While the specific prices listed will vary based on innumerable factors, the charts are instructive for first-time buyers.

The first scenario details a budget-minded keeper, trying to spend as little as possible. The second example estimates the costs for a keeper with a moderate budget, and the third example provides a case study for extravagant shoppers, who want an expensive chameleon and top-notch equipment.

These charts are only provided estimates; your experience may vary based on a variety of factors.

Inexpensive Option

Hatchling Panther Chameleon, Male	$200 (£136)
Economy Homemade Habitat	$50 (£34)
Heat Lamp Fixture and Bulbs	$20 (£13)
Full Spectrum Fixture and Bulbs	$50 (£34)
Plants, Substrate, Perches, etc.	$50 (£34)
Infrared Thermometer	$35 (£24)
Digital Indoor-Outdoor Thermometer	$20 (£13)
Water Dish, Forceps, Spray Bottles, Misc.	$25 (£17)
Total	$450 (£305)

Moderate Option

Premium Panther Chameleon, Juvenile, Male	$400 (£272)
Premium Homemade Habitat	$100 (£68)
Heat Lamp Fixture and Bulbs	$20 (£13)
Full Spectrum Fixture and Bulbs	$50 (£34)
Plants, Substrate, Perches, etc.	$50 (£34)
Infrared Thermometer	$35 (£24)
Digital Indoor-Outdoor Thermometer	$20 (£13)
Water Dish, Forceps, Spray Bottles, Misc.	$25 (£17)
Total	$700 (£475)

Premium Option

Premium Panther Chameleon, Adult, Male	$1,000 (£680)
Premium Commercial Cage	$500 (£340)
Heat Lamp and Bulbs	$20 (£13)
Full Spectrum Fixture and Bulbs	$50 (£34)
Plants, Substrate, Perches, etc.	$50 (£34)
Infrared Thermometer	$35 (£24)
Digital Indoor-Outdoor Thermometer	$20 (£13)
Water Dish, Forceps, Spray Bottles, Misc.	$25 (£17)
Total	$1700 (£1155)

Ongoing Costs

The ongoing costs of panther chameleon ownership primarily fall into one of three categories: food, maintenance and veterinary care.

Food costs are the most significant of the three, but they are relatively consistent and somewhat predictable. Some maintenance costs are easy to calculate, but things like equipment malfunctions are impossible to predict with any certainty. Veterinary expenses are hard to predict and vary wildly from one year to the next.

Food Costs

Food is the single greatest ongoing cost you will experience while caring for your chameleon. To obtain a reasonable estimate of your yearly food costs, you must consider the number of meals you will feed your pet per year and the cost of each meal.

The amount of food your chameleon consumes will vary based on numerous factors, including his size, the average temperatures in his habitat, his health and the size of the food items. However, a reasonable estimate would be in the ballpark of 10 items per feeding. If you feed your pet seven times per week, he will require 70 insects per week, or about 3500 per year.

Most common feeder insects cost between $0.01 and $0.10 cents each, depending on the species and size. Most commercially produced insects are cheaper when purchased in bulk.

Accordingly, it will cost you somewhere between $35 and $350 per year (£24 to £245) to feed your pet. This estimate spans an order of magnitude, but it remains somewhat helpful for planning your costs (it also speaks to the importance of minimizing food costs and waste).

Professional breeders utilizing efficient feeding systems and bulk purchasing power incur costs at the lower end of that range, while pet owners who purchase their insects at retail prices and fail to use them efficiently will undoubtedly find themselves at the high end of this range.

You may also provide your pet with the occasional dark leafy green or fruit, which can further increase your food costs. The actual quantity of vegetables your pet eats will remain low, but these costs can still remain significant.

Your panther chameleon may spend all week munching on a single collard green leaf, which probably costs less than a dime. However, you must obtain a leaf like that every week or so, and few grocery stores market their produce in chameleon-friendly serving sizes. Instead, you must purchase a whole head or bunch of greens, even though your pet has no chance of consuming much of it before the leaves wilt and turn brown.

Frozen and canned vegetables are largely unsuitable for lizards, so there is little you can do to avoid this problem. Accordingly, your vegetable bill may very well become significant. Even if you only spend $2.00 per week on vegetables, that amounts to over $100 (£68) each year.

One of the best ways to sidestep this problem is to grow your own vegetables for your chameleon, but this often requires space (and suitable climate) which is not always available. You may be able to talk to the produce manager at your local grocery store or farmer's market – he or she may be able to offer you individual leaves at a reasonable price.

Veterinary Costs

Unlike many other pet reptiles, who probably benefit from an annual veterinary exam, panther chameleons do not tolerate stress well, and any non-essential travel should be avoided.

While you should always seek veterinary advice at the first sign of illness, it is probably not wise to haul your healthy chameleon to the vet's office for no reason. Accordingly, you shouldn't incur any veterinary expenses unless your pet falls ill.

However, veterinary care can become very expensive, very quickly. In addition to a basic exam or phone consultation, your lizard may need cultures, x-rays or other diagnostic tests performed. In light of this, wise keepers budget at least $200 to $300 (£136 to £204) each year to cover any emergency veterinary costs.

Maintenance Costs

It is important to plan for both routine and unexpected maintenance costs. Commonly used items, such as paper towels, disinfectant and top soil are rather easy to calculate. However, it is not easy to know how many burned out light bulbs, cracked misting units or faulty thermostats you will have to replace in a given year.

Those who keep their chameleons in simple enclosures will find that about $50 (£34) covers their yearly maintenance costs. By contrast, those who maintain elaborate habitats may spend $200 (£136) or more each year.

Always try to purchase frequently used supplies, such as light bulbs, paper towels and disinfectants in bulk to maximize your savings. It is often beneficial to consult with local reptile-keeping clubs, who often pool their resources to attain greater buying power.

Myths and Misunderstandings

Myth: Chameleons change color to camouflage with their surroundings.

Fact: Chameleons change colors for a few primary reasons, but camouflage is not really one of them. Despite the way they are portrayed in popular culture, chameleons do not assume the colors and patterns surrounding them (as, for example, a cephalopod may).

The primary reasons chameleons change colors are social in nature. Males frequently display the boldest colors when they see a receptive female or a challenging male in the area.

Females display different colors depending on their reproductive condition.

Myth: Chameleons need "friends" or they will get lonely.

Fact: While a handful of chameleon species appear to thrive in small groups, panther chameleons are solitary animals that spend the bulk of their lives alone. Communally caged panther chameleons are likely to become stressed; males may engage in violent conflicts with other males or stress females with incessant breeding attempts.

Young panther chameleons often cohabitate well with each other, as long as their habitats are suitably large and feature numerous visual barriers. However, just because they will tolerate being raised in groups does not mean they enjoy it – they would much rather be in their own cage.

It is also important to point out that even chameleons that appear to be cohabitating peacefully are usually suffering from the effects of chronic stress. Their keepers simply fail to observe the subtle signs exhibited by the lizards.

Myth: Reptiles grow in proportion to the size of their cage and then stop.

Fact: Reptiles do no such thing. Most healthy lizards, snakes and turtles grow throughout their lives, although the rate of growth slows with age (a very few stop growing with maturity, although this is not influenced by the size of their cage).

Placing them in a small cage in an attempt to stunt their growth is an unthinkably cruel practice, which is more likely to sicken or kill your pet than stunt its growth.

Providing a panther chameleon with an inadequately spacious cage is a sure recipe for illness, maladaptation and eventual death.

Note the downward-facing eye of this juvenile chameleon.

Myth: Chameleons must eat live food.

Fact: While chameleons primarily hunt live prey in the wild, you can often trick them into eating pre-killed insects by holding the insect in a long pair of tongs or forceps and moving it in front of the lizard's face.

However, this is time consuming (imagine doing this ten times a day, five days a week for five or six years!), and rarely preferable to simply giving your pet live insects.

If you choose to feed your lizard vertebrate prey of any kind, you should only offer pre-killed food to avoid causing any suffering for the prey animal.

Myth: Reptiles have no emotions and do not suffer.

Fact: While chameleons have very primitive brains and do not have emotions comparable to those of higher mammals, they can absolutely suffer. Always treat reptiles with the same compassion you would offer a dog, cat or horse.

Myth: Chameleons are tame lizards that never bite.

Fact: Some chameleons bite readily when held. Although their bites are rarely serious, panther chameleons have surprisingly strong jaws for their size and can inflict a surprisingly strong pinch with their jaws.

Chameleons do possess teeth, although they are relatively short and unlikely to cause deep wounds.

Acquiring Your Panther Chameleon

Modern reptile enthusiasts can acquire panther chameleons from a variety of sources, each with a different set of pros and cons.

Pet stores are one of the first places many people see panther chameleons, and they become the de facto source of pets for many beginning keepers. While they do offer some unique benefits to prospective keepers, pet stores are not always the best place to purchase a chameleon; so, consider all of the available options, including breeders and reptile swap meets, before making a purchase.

Pet Stores

Pet stores offer a number of benefits to keepers shopping for panther chameleons, including convenience: They usually stock all of the equipment your new lizard needs, including cages, heating devices and food items.

Additionally, they offer you the chance to inspect the lizard up close before purchase. In some cases, you may be able to choose from more than one specimen. Many pet stores provide health guarantees for a short period, that provides some recourse if your new pet turns out to be ill.

However, pet stores are not always the ideal place to purchase your new pet. Pet stores are retail establishments, and as such, you will usually pay more for your new pet than you would from a breeder.

Additionally, pet stores rarely know the pedigree of the animals they sell, and they will rarely know the lizard's date of birth, or other pertinent information. Only a handful of pet stores will be able to distinguish among the various locales of panther chameleon, so specimens may also be mislabeled.

Other drawbacks associated with pet stores primarily relate to the staff's inexperience. While some pet stores concentrate on reptiles and may educate their staff about proper chameleon care, many others are provide incorrect advice to their customers.

It is also worth considering the increased exposure to pathogens that pet store animals endure, given the constant flow of animals through such facilities.

Reptile Expos
Reptile expos offer another option for purchasing a panther chameleon. Reptile expos often feature resellers, breeders and retailers in the same room, all selling various types of chameleons and other reptiles.

Often, the prices at such events are quite reasonable and you are often able to select from many different lizards. However, if you have a problem, it may be difficult to find the seller after the event is over.

Breeders
Because they usually offer unparalleled information and support to their customers, breeders are generally the best place for most novices to shop for panther chameleons. Additionally, breeders often know the species well, and are better able to help you learn the husbandry techniques necessary for success.

For those seeking a particular type of panther chameleon, breeders are often the only option. This is especially true for those seeking chameleons from underrepresented locations. The same principle holds true for those seeking spectacular individuals from proven bloodlines – the only place to purchase such chameleons are from breeders.

The primary disadvantage of buying from a breeder is that you must often make such purchases from a distance, either by phone or via the internet. Nevertheless, most established breeders are happy to provide you with photographs of the animal you will be purchasing, as well as his or her parents.

Selecting Your Chameleon

Not all chameleons are created equally, so it is important to select a healthy individual that will give you the best chance of success.

Practically speaking, the most important criterion to consider is the health of the animal. However, the sex, age and history of the lizard are also important things to consider.

Health Checklist

Always check your chameleon thoroughly for signs of injury or illness before purchasing it. If you are purchasing the animal from someone in a different part of the country, you must inspect it immediately upon delivery. Notify the seller promptly if the animal exhibits any health problems.

Avoid the temptation to acquire or accept a sick or injured animal in hopes of nursing him back to health. Not only are you likely to incur substantial veterinary costs while treating your new pet, you will likely fail in your attempts to restore the lizard to full health. Sick chameleons rarely recover in the hands of novices (or, for that matter, experts).

Additionally, by purchasing injured or diseased animals, you incentivize poor husbandry on the part of the retailer.

If retailers lose money on sick or injured animals, they will take steps to avoid this eventuality, by acquiring healthier stock in the first place, and providing better care for their charges.

As much as is possible, try to observe the following features:

- **Observe the lizard's skin**. It should be free of lacerations and other damage. Pay special attention to those areas that frequently sustain damage, such as the tip of the lizard's tail, the toes and the tip of the snout. A small cut or abrasion may be relatively easy to treat, but significant abrasions and cuts are likely to become infected and require significant treatment.

- **Gently check the lizard's crevices and creases for mites and ticks**. Mites are about the size of a flake of pepper, and they may be black, brown or red. Mites often move about on the lizard, whereas ticks – if attached and feeding – do not move. Avoid purchasing any animal that has either parasite. Additionally, you should avoid purchasing any other animals from this source, as they are likely to harbor parasites as well.

- **Examine the lizard's eyes, ears and nostrils**. The eyes should not be sunken, and they should be free of discharge. The nostrils should be clear and dry – lizards with runny noses or those who blow bubbles are likely to be suffering from a respiratory infection. However, be aware that lizards often get some water in their nostrils while drinking water. This is no cause for concern.

- **Gently palpate the animal and ensure no lumps or anomalies are apparent.** Lumps in the muscles or abdominal cavity may indicate parasites, abscesses or tumors.

- **Observe the lizard's demeanor.** Healthy lizards are aware of their environment and react to stimuli. When active, the lizard should calmly explore his environment. While you may wish to avoid purchasing an aggressive, defensive or flighty animal, these behaviors do not necessarily indicate a health problem.

- **Check the lizard's vent.** The vent should be clean and free of smeared feces. Smeared feces can indicate parasites or bacterial infections.

- **Check the lizard's appetite.** If possible, ask the retailer to feed the lizard a cricket, superworm or roach. A healthy chameleon should usually exhibit a strong food drive, although failing to eat is not *necessarily* a bad sign – the lizard may not be hungry.

The Age

Hatchling panther chameleons are very fragile until they reach about one month of age. Before this, they are unlikely to thrive in the hands of beginning keepers.

Accordingly, most beginners should purchase two- or three-month-old juveniles, who have already become well established. Animals of this age tolerate the changes associated with a new home better than very young specimens do. Further, given their greater size, they will better tolerate temperature and humidity extremes than smaller animals will.

Mature animals are rarely preferable to juveniles, as they may have become accustomed to their surroundings and fail to adapt to their new home. Experienced keepers can often navigate such a transition, but beginners are better served by purchasing a younger animal.

The Sex

Unless you are attempting to breed panther chameleons, you should select a male pet. Females not only live much shorter lives than males, but they are also more likely to suffer from reproduction-related health problems.

Most females will produce and deposit egg clutches upon reaching maturity, whether they are housed with a male or not. While this is not necessarily problematic, novices can easily avoid this unnecessary complication by selecting males as pets.

Because males bear bolder colors than females do, few keepers are resistant to this suggestion. However, the market has responded to the greater demand for males, causing them to command higher prices than females do.

This provides yet another reason to purchase two- or three-month-old juveniles rather than younger animals: Hatchling panther chameleons are very difficult to sex correctly.

Quarantine

Because new animals may have illnesses or parasites that could infect the rest of your collection, it is wise to quarantine all new acquisitions. This means that you should keep any new animal as separated from the rest of your pets as possible. Only once you have ensured that the new animal is healthy should you introduce it to the rest of your collection.

During the quarantine period, you should keep the new lizard in a simplified habitat, with a paper substrate, water bowl, basking spot and a few hiding places. Keep the temperature and humidity at ideal levels.

It is wise to obtain fecal samples from your lizard during the quarantine period. You can take these samples to your veterinarian, who can check them for signs of internal parasites. Always treat any existing parasite infestations before removing the animal from quarantine.

Always tend to quarantined animals last, as this reduces the chances of transmitting pathogens to your healthy animals. Do not wash quarantined water bowls or cage furniture with those belonging to your healthy animals. Whenever possible, use completely separate tools for quarantined animals and those that have been in your collection for some time.

Always be sure to wash your hands thoroughly after handling quarantined animals, their cages or their tools. Particularly careful keepers wear a smock or alternative clothing when handling quarantined animals.

Quarantine new acquisitions for a minimum of 30 days; 60 or 90 days is even better. Many zoos and professional breeders maintain 180- or 360-day-long quarantine periods.

Chapter 6: Providing the Captive Habitat

In most respects, providing chameleons with a suitable captive habitat entails functionally replicating the various aspects of their wild habitats.

In addition to providing your pet with an enclosure, you must provide the animal with the correct thermal environment, appropriate humidity, substrate, and suitable cage furniture.

Enclosure

Providing your chameleon with appropriate housing is and essential aspect of captive care. In essence, the habitat you provide to your pet becomes his world.

In "the old days," those inclined to keep reptiles had few choices with regard to caging. The two primary options were to build a custom cage from scratch or construct a lid to use with a fish aquarium.

By contrast, modern hobbyists have a variety of options from which to choose. In addition to building custom cages or adapting aquaria, dozens of different cage styles are available – each with different pros and cons.

Remember: There are few absolutes regarding reptile husbandry, and what works for most keepers and lizards may not work for you and your pet. Additionally, advanced keepers are often able to sidestep problems that trouble beginners.

Dimensions

Chameleons require a fair bit of space to thrive. Ideally, each adult should have an enclosure with about 6 to 8 square feet of floor space, although some keepers provide only about half of this. Hatchlings and juveniles obviously require less space than this, and females require less space than males do.

Panther chameleons appreciate a significant amount of vertical space in their cage. Minimally, they require cages with about 3 feet of vertical space, but 6-foot-tall cages are ideal.

Aquariums

Aquariums are popular choices for many pet reptiles and they are available at virtually every pet store in the country. However, they make poor enclosures for chameleons and should be avoided.

Panther chameleons (and most other commonly kept chameleon species) require a great deal of ventilation and air exchange to thrive. Those kept in poorly ventilated cages are highly susceptible to respiratory infections.

Additionally, because of their glass construction, aquariums often create reflections. When your pet sees their reflection, they take it to be a conspecific, and they react accordingly.

Constantly living in close proximity to another panther chameleon (perceived or real) leads to stress, which can lead to health problems.

Commercial Cages

Commercially produced reptile enclosures (such as those designed for snakes) typically present the same challenge that aquaria do -- poor ventilation. Additionally, because most of these cages feature glass or acrylic doors, reflections can also be a problem.

However, in theory, such cages may work if they provide enough ventilation and reflections are not a problem.

Screened Cages

Screen cages are the gold standard of chameleon keeping. They permit plenty of air exchange with the outside world and produce none of the stress-causing reflections that are common in aquariums.

You can purchase pre-built screen cages or construct your own. A variety of styles have been used successfully, and each has its own benefits and drawbacks.

Opt for plastic-coated screening whenever possible, as tightly woven, metal screens may catch the toenails of large animals, leading to injury. However, insects will readily escape from cages with wide mesh, so you must balance these competing interests.

A final benefit offered by screen cages is their low price. Relative to cages made of wood, glass or plastic, screen cages are inexpensive.

Plastic Storage Containers

Plastic storage containers, such as those used for shoes, sweaters or food, are popular enclosure options for many reptiles, but they are poorly suited for chameleons. The reasons for this primarily relate to the poor ventilation offered by these containers.

Nevertheless, some breeders use plastic storage containers (or large plastic buckets) to contain small groups of young chameleons. Under the watchful eye of an experienced keeper, such strategies may work, but they represent an inappropriate approach for most beginners.

Usually, to make such systems work, the containers must be tall enough to contain the lizards without the need for a lid. Obviously, this is not advisable in homes with pets or small children.

Semi-Free Range
Some keepers embrace husbandry methods that use no enclosure at all.

For example, you can set up a small room as your chameleon's habitat by strategically placing trees, plants, perches and lighting facilities in an otherwise empty room.

Because of their tendency to hang out "in the open," it is rarely hard to locate your lizard. Nevertheless, care must be taken to prevent them from escaping or accessing anything that may harm them.

You could also set a large houseplant (such as a fig tree) in a large plastic bucket and use the tree as the lizard's "cage." If set up correctly, the lizard will be unlikely to leave the tree, and unable to scale the sides of the bucket.

Chapter 7: Establishing the Thermal Environment

Providing the proper thermal environment is one of the most important aspects of reptile husbandry. As ectothermic ("cold blooded") animals, chameleons rely on the surrounding temperatures to regulate the rate at which their metabolism operates.

Providing a proper thermal environment can mean the difference between a healthy, thriving chameleon and one who spends a great deal of time at the veterinarian's office, battling infections and illness.

While individuals may demonstrate slightly different preferences, active panther chameleons generally prefer ambient temperatures in the low 80s Fahrenheit (about 29 degrees Celsius). Inactive (sleeping) chameleons prefer temperatures in the high 60s to low 70s Fahrenheit (20 to 22 degrees Celsius).

Chameleons are not helpless outside of their preferred temperature range, and they can remain active for brief periods at temperatures ranging from the low 60s to the low 90s (about 18 to 32 degrees Celsius). Indeed nighttime temperatures lower than these are unlikely to be problematic as long as the lizard is afforded access to suitably warm temperatures during the day.

When the ambient temperatures are outside of their preferred range, panther chameleons adjust their behavior to bring their body temperature into the preferred range. For example, a panther chameleon may turn his side toward the sun and display dark colors to help absorb as much solar radiation as possible. Conversely, panther chameleons cope with uncomfortably warm temperatures by retreating to the shade or gaping their mouths.

Providing your chameleon with a suitable thermal environment requires the correct approach, the correct heating equipment and the tools necessary for monitoring the thermal environment.

Size-Related Heating Concerns

Before examining the best way to establish a proper thermal environment, it is important to understand that your lizard's body size influences the way in which he heats up and cools off.

Because volume increases more quickly than surface area does with increasing body size, small individuals experience more rapid temperature fluctuations than larger individuals do.

This principle is an especially important factor to keep in mind when caring for hatchling and juvenile chameleons: Thermal stress affects such lizards quickly, and excessively high temperatures often prove fatal.

Accordingly, it is imperative to protect small individuals from temperature extremes. Conversely, larger chameleons are more tolerant of temperature extremes than smaller individuals are.

Thermal Gradients

In the wild, panther chameleons move between different microhabitats so that they can maintain ideal body temperature as much as possible. You want to provide similar opportunities for your captive chameleon by creating a thermal gradient.

The best way to do this is by clustering the heating devices at one end of the habitat, thereby creating a basking spot (the warmest spot in the enclosure).

The temperatures will slowly drop with increasing distance from the basking spot, which creates a *gradient* of temperatures. Barriers, such as branches and vegetation, also help to create shaded patches, which provide additional thermal options.

This mimics the way temperatures vary from one small place to the next in your pet's natural habitat. For example, a wild chameleon may move into dense clusters of leaves to get out of the noon sun, or move onto exposed branches to warm up in the morning.

By establishing a gradient in the enclosure, your captive chameleon will be able to access a range of different temperatures, which will allow him to manage his body temperature just as his wild counterparts do.

Use care to aim the heating devices at one or more perches in such a way that your chameleon can easily access the warming rays. Thermal gradients are usually oriented horizontally in most reptile habitats, but because most chameleon cages are quite tall, the gradient also functions vertically.

You can place the heating devices directly above the habitat, but as wild chameleons probably bask more often in the morning and afternoon, it makes better sense to place the heating devices in such a way that they cast diagonal, rather than strictly vertical, rays.

Adjust the heating device until the surface temperatures at the basking spot are between 90 and 95 degrees Fahrenheit (32 to 35 degrees Celsius). Provide a slightly cooler basking spot for immature individuals, with maximum temperatures of about 92 degrees Fahrenheit (33 degrees Celsius). Ambient temperatures at the basking spot should be between 80 and 90 degrees Fahrenheit (26 to 32 degrees Celsius).

Because there is no heat source at the other end of the cage, the ambient temperature will gradually fall as your lizard moves away from the heat source. Ideally, the cool end of the cage should be in the low 70s Fahrenheit (22 degrees Celsius).

The need to establish a thermal gradient is one of the most compelling reasons to use a large cage. In general, the larger the cage, the easier it is to establish a suitable thermal gradient.

Heating Equipment

Heat lamps are likely the best choices for supplying heat to your chameleon. Heat lamps consist of a reflector dome and an incandescent bulb. The light bulb produces heat (in addition to light) and the metal reflector dome directs the heat to a spot inside the cage.

You will need to clamp the lamp to a stable anchor or part of the cage's frame. Always be sure that the lamp is securely attached and will not be dislodged by vibration, children or pets.

Because fire safety is always a concern, and many keepers use high-wattage lightbulbs, opt for heavy-duty reflector domes with ceramic bases, rather than economy units with plastic bases. The price difference is negligible, given the stakes.

One of the greatest benefits of using heat lamps to maintain the temperature of your pet's habitat is the flexibility they offer. While you can adjust the amount of heat provided by heat tapes and other devices with a rheostat or thermostat, you can adjust the enclosure temperature provided by heat lamps in two ways:

- **Changing the Bulb Wattage**

The simplest way to adjust the temperature of your chameleon's cage is by changing the wattage of the bulb you are using. For example, if a 40-watt light bulb is not raising the temperature of the basking spot high enough, you may try a 60-watt bulb. Alternatively, if a 100-watt light bulb is elevating the cage temperatures higher than are appropriate, switching to a 60-watt bulb may help.

- **Adjusting the Distance between the Heat Lamp and the Basking Spot**

The closer the heat lamp is to the cage, the warmer the cage will be. If the habitat is too warm, you can move the light farther from the enclosure, which should lower the basking spot temperatures slightly.

However, the farther away you move the lamp, the larger the basking spot becomes. It is important to be careful that you do not move it to far away, which will reduce the effectiveness of the thermal gradient by heating the enclosure too uniformly. In very large cages, this may not compromise the thermal gradient very much, but in a small cage, it may eliminate the "cool side" of the habitat.

In other words, if your heat lamp creates a basking spot that is roughly 1-foot in diameter when it is 1inch away from the screen, it will produce a slightly cooler, but larger basking spot when moved back another 6 inches or so.

Nocturnal Temperatures

Because panther chameleon's safely tolerate temperatures in the high-60s Fahrenheit (20 degrees Celsius) at night, most keepers can allow their panther chameleon's habitat to fall to ambient room temperature at night.

Because it is important to avoid using lights on your chameleon's habitat at night, those living in homes with lower nighttime temperatures will need to employ additional heat sources. Most such keepers accomplish this through the use of ceramic heat emitters.

Ceramic heat emitters are small devices that function as light bulbs do, except that they do not produce any visible light – they only produce heat. While they are not an ideal heat source for your chameleon's daytime basking needs, they are very helpful for keeping your pet suitably warm at night.

You can use ceramic heat emitters in reflector-dome fixtures, just as you would use incandescent bulbs.

Thermometers

It is important to monitor the cage temperatures very carefully to ensure your pet stays health. Just as a water test kit is an aquarist's best friend, quality thermometers are some of the most important husbandry tools for reptile keepers.

Ambient and Surface Temperatures

Two different types of temperature are relevant for pet lizards: ambient temperatures and surface temperatures.

The ambient temperature in your animal's enclosure is the air temperature; the surface temperatures are the temperatures of the objects in the cage. Both are important to monitor, as they can differ widely.

For example, the air temperatures may be 90 degrees Fahrenheit (32 degrees Celsius) on a hot summer day, but the surface of a black rock may be in excess of 120 degrees Fahrenheit (48 degrees Celsius).

A lizard may comfortably rest on a branch with a surface temperature of 100 degrees Fahrenheit (37 degrees Celsius), but suffer from extreme heat stress if exposed to ambient temperatures in this range for very long.

Conversely, 150-degree ambient temperatures may be fatal, but they won't burn your lizard's skin. On the other hand, 150-degree surface temperatures may very well burn your pet's skin.

Measure the cage's ambient temperatures with a digital thermometer. An indoor-outdoor model will feature a probe that allows you to measure the temperature at both ends of the thermal gradient at once. For example, you may position the thermometer at the cool side of the cage, but attach the remote probe to a branch near the basking spot.

Because standard digital thermometers do not measure surface temperatures well, use a non-contact, infrared thermometer for such measurements. These devices will allow you to measure surface temperatures accurately from a short distance away.

Chapter 8: Lighting the Enclosure

Given the amount of time they spend hanging out in the tropical sun, it should come as no surprise that panther chameleons have evolved to depend upon it. It is always preferable to afford captive chameleons access to unfiltered sunlight, but this is not always possible. In these cases, it is necessary to provide your chameleon with high quality lighting, which can partially satisfy their need for real sunlight.

Chameleons deprived of appropriate lighting may become seriously ill. Learning how to provide the proper lighting for reptiles is sometimes an arduous task for beginners, but it is very important to the long-term health of your pet that you do. To understand the type of light your lizard needs, you must first understand a little bit about light.

Light is a type of energy that physicists call electromagnetic radiation; it travels in waves. These waves may differ in amplitude, which correlates to the vertical distance between consecutive wave crests and troughs, frequency, which correlates with the number of crests per unit of time, and wavelength.

Wavelength is the distance from one crest to the next, or one trough to the next. Wavelength and frequency are inversely proportional, meaning that as the wavelength increases, the frequency decreases. It is more common for reptile keepers to discuss wavelengths rather than frequencies.

The sun produces energy (light) with a very wide range of constituent wavelengths. Some of these wavelengths fall within a range called the visible spectrum; humans can detect these rays with their eyes. Such waves have wavelengths between about 390 and 700 nanometers. Rays with wavelengths longer or shorter than these limits are broken into their own groups and given different names.

Those rays with around 390 nanometer wavelengths or less are called ultraviolet rays or UV rays. UV rays are broken down into three different categories, just as the different colors correspond with different wavelengths of visible light. UVA rays have wavelengths between 315 to 400 nanometers, while UVB rays have wavelengths between 280 and 315 nanometers while UVC rays have wavelengths between 100 and 280 nanometers.

Rays with wavelengths of less than 280 nanometers are called x-rays and gamma rays. At the other end of the spectrum, infrared rays have wavelengths longer than 700 nanometers; microwaves and radio waves are even longer.

UVA rays are important for food recognition, appetite, activity and eliciting natural behaviors. UVB rays are necessary for many reptiles to produce vitamin D3. Without this vitamin, reptiles cannot properly metabolize their calcium.

The light that comes from the sun and light bulbs is composed of a combination of wavelengths, which create the blended white light that you perceive. This combination of wavelengths varies slightly from one light source to the next.

The sun produces very balanced white light, while "economy" incandescent bulbs produce relatively fewer blue rays and yields a yellow-looking light. High-quality bulbs designed for reptiles often produce very balanced, white light. The degree to which light causes objects to look as they would under sunlight is called the Color Rendering Index, or CRI. Sunlight has a CRI of 100, while quality bulbs have CRIs of 80 to 90; by contrast, a typical incandescent bulb has a CRI of 40 to 50

Another important characteristic of light that relates to chameleons is luminosity, or the brightness of light. Measured in units called Lux, luminosity is an important consideration for your lighting system. While you cannot possibly replicate the intensity of the sun's light, it is desirable in most circumstances to ensure the habitat is lit as well as is reasonably possible.

For example, in the tropics, the sunlight intensity averages around 100,000 Lux at midday; by comparison, the lights in a typical family living room only produce about 50 Lux.

Without bright lighting, many reptiles become lethargic, depressed or exhibit hibernating behaviors. Dim lighting may inhibit feeding and cause lizards to become stressed and ill.

To summarize, chameleons and most other lizards require:

- Light that is comprised of visible light, as well as UVA and UVB wavelengths
- Light with a high color-rendering index
- Light of the sufficiently strong intensity

Now that you know what your lizard requires, you can go about designing the lighting system for his habitat. Ultraviolet radiation is the most difficult component of proper lighting to provide, so it makes sense to begin by examining the types of bulbs that produce UV radiation.

The only commercially produced bulbs that produce significant amounts of UVA and UVB and suitable for a chameleon habitat are linear fluorescent light bulbs, compact fluorescent light bulbs and mercury vapor bulbs.

Neither type of fluorescent bulb produces significant amounts of heat, but mercury vapor bulbs produce a lot of heat and serve a dual function. In many cases, keepers elect to use both types of lights – a mercury vapor bulb for a warm basking site with high levels of UV radiation and fluorescent bulbs to light the rest of the cage without raising the temperature. You can also use fluorescent bulbs to provide the requisite UV radiation and use a regular incandescent bulb to generate the basking spot.

Fluorescent bulbs have a much longer history of use than mercury vapor bulbs, which makes some keepers more comfortable using them. However, many models only produce moderate amounts of UVB radiation. While some mercury vapor bulbs produce significant quantities of UVB, some question the wisdom of producing more UV radiation than the animal receives in the wild. Additionally, mercury vapor bulbs are much too powerful to use in small habitats, and they are more expensive initially.

Most fluorescent bulbs must be placed within 12 inches of the basking surface, while some mercury vapor bulbs should be placed farther away from the basking surface – be sure to read the manufacturer's instructions before use.

Be sure that the bulbs you purchase specifically state the amount of UVB radiation they produce; this figure is expressed as a percentage, for example 7% UVB. Most UVB-producing bulbs require replacement every six to 12 months – whether or not they have stopped producing light.

However, ultraviolet radiation is only one of the characteristics that lizard keepers must consider. The light bulbs used must also produce a sunlight-like spectrum. Fortunately, most high-quality light bulbs that produce significant amounts of UVA and UVB radiation also feature a high color-rendering index. The higher the CRI, the better, but any bulbs with a CRI of 90 or above will work well. If you are having trouble deciding between two otherwise evenly matched bulbs, select the one with the higher CRI value.

Brightness is the final, and easiest, consideration for the keeper to address. While no one yet knows what the ideal luminosity for a chameleon's cage, it makes sense to ensure that at least part of the cage features very bright lighting. However, you should always offer a shaded retreat within the enclosure into which your lizard can avoid the light if he desires.

Connect the lights to an electric timer to keep the length of the day and night consistent. Some breeders manipulate their captive's photoperiod over the course of the year to prime the animals for breeding, but pet chameleons thrive with 12 hours of daylight and 12 hours of darkness all year long.

Readers are encouraged to review (Gary W. Ferguson, 2002) for further information on the ultraviolet lighting requirements of panther chameleons.

Chapter 9: Substrate and Furniture

Once you have purchased or constructed your chameleon's enclosure, you must place appropriate items inside it. In general, these items take the form of an appropriate substrate and the proper cage furniture, including live plants and numerous perches.

Substrate

Substrate is a contentious issue among chameleon keepers. Some keepers utilize substrates similar to those used by keepers of other lizards, while others prefer to keep the cage floor bare. Both approaches have their merits.

Bare Enclosure Floors (No Substrate)

If you are using an enclosure with a plastic, glass or laminated floor, you can avoid using any substrate at all. The primary benefit to this approach is that you do not have to worry about your pet inadvertently ingesting some of the substrate during feeding activities. Of course, if you provide your pet's food in a food cup, this is not a problem anyway.

By skipping the substrate, you can also avoid having to replace it periodically as well as the small associated expense. However, substrate-free maintenance requires more maintenance, as the cage bottom must be cleaned daily.

One drawback to substrate-free husbandry is that water will begin to pool on the cage floor if you mist the cage. This can be messy and accelerate the growth of bacterial colonies.

Substrate-free maintenance is best suited for maintaining hatchlings and juveniles, particularly when they are housed in groups. This approach allows the keeper to avoid the use of feeding cups, while reducing the chances that the hatchlings will ingest substrate.

Cypress Mulch

Cypress mulch is a popular substrate choice for panther chameleons. It not only looks attractive and holds humidity well, but cypress mulch typically has a pleasant odor.

One drawback to cypress mulch is that some brands (or individual bags among otherwise good brands) produce a stick-like mulch, rather than mulch composed of thicker pieces. These sharp sticks can injure the keeper and the kept. It usually only takes one cypress mulch splinter jammed under a keeper's fingernail to cause them to switch substrates.

Cypress mulch does represent an ingestion hazard, so keepers using it should always offer food via a feeding cup. Additionally, the numerous nooks and crannies produced by the mulch will provide insects with places to hide.

Cypress mulch is available from most home improvement and garden centers, as well as pet supply retailers. No matter the source you use, be sure that the product contains 100 percent cypress mulch without any demolition or salvage content.

Fir (Orchid) Bark

The bark of fir trees is often used for orchid propagation, and so it is often called "orchid bark." Orchid bark is very attractive, and, thanks to its relatively uniform shape, does not represent as much of an ingestion hazard as cypress mulch does. However, it is still wise to use a feeding cup if you elect to cover the bottom of the cage with this substrate.

Orchid bark absorbs water very well, so it is useful for species that require high humidity, such as panther chameleons. Additionally, orchid bark is easy to spot clean. However, monthly replacement can be expensive for those living in the Eastern United States and Europe.

Soils

Soil is another acceptable substrate for panther chameleons. You can make a suitable soil substrate by digging up your own soil, purchasing organic soil products or mixing your own blend.

Soil is a great substrate choice for those who intend to breed their chameleons – if the moisture level is appropriate and the soil has enough depth, females will bury their eggs directly in the cage substrate.

Avoid products containing perlite, manure, fertilizers, pre-emergent herbicides or other additives. Sterilization of the soil before adding it to the enclosure is not strictly necessary; in fact, many of the microorganisms present will help breakdown waste products from your lizard.

Paper Products

Newspaper, paper towels and commercial cage liners are acceptable for use with panther chameleons, but they offer few benefits over a bare floor. The only real benefit paper substrates offer chameleon keepers is that they make it easier to clean the cage floor – you can simply remove the paper each day and replace it with a fresh sheet.

However, paper substrates give insects places to hide, which means that you should use a feeding cup with paper substrates.

Substrate Comparison Chart

Substrate	Pros	Cons
No Substrate	No ingestion hazard. Easy to spot clean and sterilize. Free.	Unattractive. Water pools on surface.
Soil	Absorbs and retains water and easy to spot clean.	Ingestion hazard. Messy.
Cypress Mulch	Absorbs and retains water, attractive and easy to spot clean.	Ingestion hazard. Messy. Provides hiding places for insects.
Fir (Orchid) Bark	Absorbs and retains water, attractive and easy to spot clean.	Ingestion hazard. Messy. Provides hiding places for insects. Expensive.
Newspaper	Absorbs *some* water. Safe, low-cost. Easy to maintain and keep clean.	Unattractive. Provides hiding places for insects.
Commercial	Absorbs *some*	Provides hiding

Substrate	Pros	Cons
Paper Products	water. Safe, low-cost. Easy to maintain and keep clean.	places for insects. Can be expensive.

Substrates to Avoid

Some substrates are completely inappropriate for chameleon maintenance, and should be avoided at all costs. These include:

- **Aspen or Pine Shavings** – Wood shavings (as opposed to shredded bark or mulch) are not appropriate substrates for panther chameleons. In addition to representing a choking hazard, wood shavings will quickly rot if they become wet.

- **Cedar Shavings** – Cedar shavings produce toxic fumes that may sicken or kill your chameleon. Always avoid cedar shavings.

- **Sand** – Sand is too dusty for panther chameleons. It will also stick to feeder insects and your chameleon's tongue, where it will find its way into your lizard's digestive tract.

- **Gravel** – You can use large gravel as a substrate, but its problems outweigh its benefits. Gravel must be washed when soiled, which is laborious and time consuming. Gravel is also quite heavy, which can cause headaches for the keeper.

- **Artificial Turf** – Although it seems like a viable option with a number of benefits, artificial turf is not a good substrate for chameleons. Keeping artificial turf clean is difficult, and the threads may come loose and wrap around your lizard's tail, tongue or toes.

Cage Furniture

To complete your panther chameleon's habitat, you must provide him with visual barriers to help keep his stress level low, and perches, which he can use to travel through his cage.

The easiest way to provide visual barriers for your chameleon is by keeping live plants in the enclosure. In addition to providing a place for your pet to slip out of sight, live plants increase the humidity of the enclosure. Some plants can also provide enough perching opportunities that you needn't use any additional perches in the enclosure.

However, most keepers will find it necessary to provide perches so that their pet can access all areas of the cage. All perches must be safe, easy to clean and securely attached to the enclosure. Most keepers opt for real branches, but you can also use commercially produced plastic vines or branches.

Plants

Always wash all plants before placing them in the enclosure to help remove any pesticide residues. It is also wise to discard the potting soil used for the plant and replace it with fresh soil, which you know contains no pesticides, perlite or fertilizer.

While you can plant cage plants directly in soil substrates, this complicates maintenance and makes it difficult to replace the substrate regularly. Accordingly, it is generally preferable to keep the plant in some type of container. Be sure to use a catch tray under the pot, so that water draining from the container does not flow into the cage.

You must use care to select a species that will thrive in your chameleon's enclosure. For example, species that require direct sunlight will perish in the relatively dim light in your chameleon's enclosure.

Instead, you must choose plants that will thrive in shaded conditions. Similarly, because you will be misting the cage regularly, and trying to keep the internal environment as humid as possible, few succulents or other plants adapted to arid habitats will live in a panther chameleon enclosure.

You must also consider the growth habit and characteristics of the plants you intend to use. For example, ground covers will not prove of much use to arboreal lizards. You need plants that not only grow vertically, but you need plants that provide comfortable perching opportunities for the lizards. The plants should also have broad leaves, which will allow them to serve as visual barriers and also provide a good surface from which your chameleon will drink water. They must also

Panther chameleons may chew on the leaves of the plants in their enclosure, so it is wise to restrict your choices to non-toxic plants. The problem is that there is no widespread agreement about which plants are toxic to reptiles; most of the available literature concerns plants that are toxic to dogs and cats.

Nevertheless, many panther chameleons have been observed eating the leaves of devil's ivy (*Pothos* spp.) plants, which contain calcium oxalates that may irritate the digestive system and mouth of dogs and cats, and fig leaves (*Ficus* spp.), which have sap that is harmful to some dogs and cats.

While both of these plants are sometimes safe for use with panther chameleon (fig trees occasionally cause panther chameleons to develop eye problems), it is unwise to take unnecessary risks.

It is also worth mentioning that there are numerous species of fig trees, and those sold in retail establishments do not always bear complete (or correct) identifications. Some species may be problematic for panther chameleons, while others are perfectly fine.

Because every panther chameleon is an individual and capable of reacting differently to a given plant, it is impossible to guarantee the safety of any species. Always consult with your veterinarian before selecting plants for the enclosure.

Some of the most common choices that are likely safe and well suited for your panther chameleon's enclosures include:

- Devil's Ivy (*Pothos* spp.)
- White mulberry (*Morus alba*)
- Fig trees (*Ficus* spp.)
- Hibiscus (*Hibiscus* spp.)
- Winged elms (*Ulmus alata*)
- American elms (*Ulmus americana*)
- Black willows (*Salix nigra*)

- Umbrella tree (*Schefflera arboricola*)
- Maples (*Acer* spp.)
- Crabapple (*Malus* spp.)
- Cottonwood (Populus deltoids)
- Grape vine (*Vitis* spp.)
- Pawpaw (*Asimina* spp.)
- Honeysuckle (*Lonicera* spp.)

Perches

You can purchase climbing branches from pet and craft stores, or you can collect them yourself. When collecting your own branches, try to use branches that are still attached to trees (always obtain permission first). Such branches will harbor fewer insects and other invertebrate pests than dead branches will.

Many different types of branches can be used in panther chameleon cages. Most non-aromatic hardwoods suffice. See the chart below for specific recommendations.

Whenever collecting wood to be used as perches, bring a ruler so that you can visualize how large the branch will be, once it is back in the cage. Leave several inches of spare material at each end of the branch; this way, you can cut the perch to the correct length, once you arrive back home.

Always wash branches with plenty of hot water and a stiff, metal-bristled scrub brush to remove as much dirt, dust and fungus as possible before placing them in your chameleon's cage. Clean stubborn spots with a little bit of dish soap, but be sure to rinse them thoroughly afterwards.

It is also advisable to sterilize branches before placing them in a cage. The easiest way to do so is by placing the branch in a 300-degree oven for about 15 minutes. Doing so should kill the vast majority of pests and pathogens lurking inside the wood.

Some keepers like to cover their branches with a water-sealing product. This is acceptable if a non-toxic product is used and the branches are allowed to air dry for several days before being placed in the cage. However, as branches are relatively easy to replace, it is not necessary to seal them if you plan to replace them.

When placing the perches in the cage, be sure to do so in a way that allows your pet to access all areas of the cage. Make sure at least one of the perches allows him to access dense vegetation, his feeding cup and a good place to drink water. Try to strike a good balance between offering your pet plenty of perches, without overly crowding the habitat.

You can often place branches diagonally across the enclosure, in such a way that alleviates the need for direct attachment to the cage. However, horizontal branches will require secure points of attachment so they do not fall and injure your pet.

You can attach the branches to the cage in a variety of different ways. Be sure to make it easy to remove the branches as necessary, so you can clean them or transfer your lizard without having to handle him.

You can use hooks and eye-screws to suspend branches, which allows for quick and easy removal, but it is only applicable for cages with walls that will accept and support the eye-screws. You can also make "closet rod holders" by cutting a slot into small PVC caps, which are attached to the cage frame.

Recommended Tree Species for Perches

Recommended Species	Species to Avoid
Maple trees (*Acer* spp.)	**Cherry trees** (*Prunus* spp.)
Oak trees (*Quercus* spp.)	**Pine trees** (*Pinus* spp.)
Walnut trees (*Juglans* spp.)	**Cedar trees** (*Cedrus* spp., etc.)
Ash trees (*Fraxinus* spp.)	**Juniper trees** (*Juniperus* spp.)
Dogwood trees (*Cornus* spp.)	**Poison ivy / oak** (*Toxicodendron* spp.)
Sweetgum trees (*Liquidambar stryaciflua*)	
Crepe Myrtle trees (*Lagerstroemia* spp.)	
Willow trees (*Salix* spp.)	
Tuliptrees (*Liriodendron tulipifera*)	
Pear trees (*Pyrus* spp.)	
Apple trees (*Malus* spp.)	
Manzanitas (*Arctostaphylos* spp.)	
Grapevine (*Vitis* spp.)	

Chapter 10: Maintaining the Captive Habitat

Now that you have acquired your lizard and set up the enclosure, you must develop a protocol for maintaining his habitat. While chameleon habitats require major maintenance every month or so, they only require minor daily maintenance.

In addition to designing a husbandry protocol, you must embrace a record-keeping system to track your chameleon's growth and health.

Cleaning and Maintenance Procedures

Once you have decided on the proper enclosure for your pet, you must keep your lizard fed, hydrated and ensure that the habitat stays in proper working order to keep your captive healthy and comfortable.

Some tasks must be completed each day, while others are should be performed weekly, monthly or annually.

Daily

- Monitor the ambient and surface temperatures of the habitat.
- Provide drinking water (many keepers provide drinking water twice or thrice per day).
- Spot clean the cage to remove any loose insects, feces, urates or pieces of shed skin.
- Ensure that the lights, latches and other moving parts are in working order.

- Verify that your lizard is acting normally and appears healthy. You do not necessarily need to handle him to do so.
- Feed your lizard about 10 insects (some keepers only feed their captive five or six times per week).
- Ensure that the humidity and ventilation are at appropriate levels.

Weekly
- Change sheet-like substrates (newspaper, paper towels, etc.).
- Clean the inside surfaces of the enclosure.
- Inspect your lizard closely for any signs of injury, parasites or illness.
- Wash and sterilize all food dishes.

Monthly
- Break down the cage completely, remove and discard particulate substrates.
- Sterilize drip containers and similar equipment in a mild bleach solution.
- Measure and weigh your lizard.
- Photograph your pet (recommended, but not imperative).
- Prune any plants as necessary.

Annually
- Replace the batteries in your thermometers and any other devices that use them.
- Replace any UVB-producing bulbs (some must be changed every six months).

Cleaning your lizard's cage and furniture is relatively simple. Regardless of the way it became soiled, the basic process remains the same:

1. Rinse the object
2. Using a scrub brush or sponge and soapy water, remove any organic debris from the object.
3. Rinse the object thoroughly.
4. Disinfect the object.
5. Re-rinse the object.
6. Dry the object.

Chemicals & Tools

A variety of chemicals and tools are necessary for reptile care. Save yourself some time by purchasing dedicated cleaning products and keeping them in the same place that you keep your tools.

Spray Bottles

Misting your chameleon and his habitat with fresh water is one of the best ways to provide him with water. You can do this with a small, handheld misting bottle or a larger, pressurized unit (such as those used to spray herbicides). Automated units are available, but they are rarely cost-effective unless you are caring for a large colony of chameleons.

Scrub Brushes or Sponges

It helps to have a few different types of scrub brushes and sponges on hand for scrubbing and cleaning different items. Use the least abrasive sponge or brush suitable for the task to prevent wearing out cage items prematurely. Do not use abrasive materials on glass or acrylic surfaces. Steel-bristled brushes work well for scrubbing coarse, wooden items, such as branches.

Spatulas and Putty Knives

Spatulas, putty knives and similar tools are often helpful for cleaning reptile cages. For example, urates (which are not soluble in anything short of hot lava) often become stuck on cage walls or furniture. Instead of trying to dissolve them with harsh chemicals, just scrape them away with a sturdy plastic putty knife.

Small Vacuums

Small, handheld vacuums are very helpful for sucking up the dust left behind from substrates. They are also helpful for cleaning the cracks and crevices around the cage doors. A shop vacuum, with suitable hoses and attachments, can also be helpful.

Steam Cleaners

Steam cleaners are very effective for sterilizing cages, water bowls and durable cage props after they have been cleaned. In fact, steam is often a better choice than chemical disinfectants, as it will not leave behind a toxic residue. Never use a steam cleaner near your lizard, the plants in his cage or any other living organisms.

Soap

Use a gentle, non-scented dish soap. Antibacterial soap is preferred, but not necessary. Most people use far more soap than is necessary -- a few drops mixed with a quantity of water is usually sufficient to help remove surface pollutants.

Bleach

Bleach (diluted to one-half cup per gallon of water) makes an excellent disinfectant. Be careful not to spill any on clothing, carpets or furniture, as it is likely to discolor the objects.

Always be sure to rinse objects thoroughly after using bleach and be sure that you cannot detect any residual odor. Bleach does not work as a disinfectant when in contact with organic substances; accordingly, items must be cleaned before you can disinfect them.

Veterinarian Approved Disinfectant

Many commercial products are available that are designed to be safe for their pets. Consult with your veterinarian about the best product for your situation, its method of use and its proper dilution.

Avoid Phenols

Always avoid cleaners that contain phenols, as they are extremely toxic to some reptiles. In general, do not use household cleaning products to avoid exposing your pet to toxic chemicals.

Keeping Records

It is important to keep records regarding your pet's health, growth and feeding, as well as any other important details. In the past, reptile keepers would do so on small index cards or in a notebook. In the modern world, technological solutions may be easier. For example, you can use your computer or mobile device to keep track of the pertinent info about your pet.

You can record as much information about your pet as you like, and the more information to you record, the better. But minimally, you should record the following:

Pedigree and Origin Information

Be sure to record the source of your lizard, the date on which you acquired him and any other data that is available. Breeders will often provide customers with information regarding the sire, dam, date of birth, weights and feeding records, but other sources will rarely offer comparable data.

Feeding Information

Record the date of each feeding (and time of day, if you feed more than once each day), as well as the type of food item(s) offered. It is also helpful to record any preferences you may observe or any meals that are refused.

Weights and Length

Because you look at your pet frequently, it is difficult to appreciate how quickly he is (or isn't) growing. Accordingly, it is important to track his size diligently.

Weigh chameleons with a high quality digital scale. The scale must be sensitive to one-tenth-gram increments to be useful for very small lizards.

It is often easiest to use a dedicated "weighing container" with a known weight to measure your chameleon. This way, you will not have to keep the lizard stationary on the scale's platform – you can simply place him in the container and place the entire container on the scale. Subtract the weight of the container to obtain the weight of your lizard.

If you are able to incorporate removable perches in the cage, record the weight of the perch so that you can simply manipulate the chameleon's perch rather than having to pry your lizard from his perch. Just weigh the lizard on his perch, subtract the weight of the perch and record the difference as the lizard's weight.

You can measure your lizard's length as well, but it is often difficult to obtain satisfactory results with chameleons. Because chameleons typically keep their tails curled, and you should avoid manipulating your pet's tail, it is difficult to obtain an accurate total length. Instead, you can measure its snout-to-vent-length, which can be accomplished without having to handle the lizard very much.

Maintenance Information
Record all of the noteworthy events associated with your pet's care. While it is not necessary to note that you misted the cage each day, it is appropriate to record the dates on which you changed the substrate or sterilized the cage.

Whenever you purchase new equipment, supplies or caging, note the date and source. This not only helps to remind you when you purchased the items, but it may help you track down a source for the items in the future, if necessary.

Breeding Information
If you intend to breed your lizard, you should record all details associated with pre-breeding conditioning, cycling, introductions, matings, color changes, copulations and egg deposition.

Juvenile chameleons can be kept in small groups.
Picture credit: Belizar, Dreamstime

Record all pertinent information about any resulting clutches as well, including the number of viable eggs, as well as the number of unhatched and unfertilized eggs (often called "slugs" by reptile keepers).

Record Keeping Samples

The following are two different examples of suitable recording systems.

The first example is reminiscent of the style employed by many with large collections. Because such keepers often have numerous animals, the notes are very simple, and require a minimum amount of writing or typing.

ID Number: 44522		Genus: Species/Sub:	Furcifer pardalis	Gender: DOB:	Male 3/20/ 15	CAR D #2
6.30.15 Crickets	7.03.15 Crickets, Superworms	7.08.15 Large grasshopper	7.14.15 Crickets	7.17.15 Crickets		
7.01.15 Crickets	7.05.15 Crickets	7.09.15 Roaches	7.15.15 Superwo rms, Roaches	7.19.15 Sterilized Cage		
7.02.15 Roaches	7.06.15 Crickets	7.12.15 Crickets	7.16.15 Crickets			

The second example demonstrates a simple approach that is employed by many with small collections (or a single pet): keeping notes on paper. Such notes could be taken in a notebook or journal, or you could type directly into a word processor. It does not matter *how* you keep records, just that you *do* keep records.

Date	Notes
4-22-13	Acquired ""Louie" the panther chameleon from a lizard breeder named Mark at the in-town reptile expo. Mark explained that Louie's scientific name is Furcifer pardalis. Cost was $250. Mark was not sure what sex Louie was. Mark said he purchased the lizard in March, but he does not know the exact date.
4-23-13	I have decided to consider Louie a boy until he gets big enough to know for sure. He spent the night in the container I bought him in. I purchased a small screened cage, full spectrum lamp and heat lamp at the pet store. Bought the thermometer at the hardware store next door and ordered a non-contact thermometer online. I am using old food containers for his cricket cup. I added a pothos plant I bought at the hardware store.
6-27-13	Louie eagerly drank when I misted him. He ate at least 10 crickets.
6-30-13	I fed Louie 10 crickets and a big roach today. I think I need longer tweezers! His tongue is so long!
7-1-13	Since Louie looked hungry, I fed him another few roaches today.
7-3-13	Fed Louie a dozen crickets and a moth that flew into the house. He ate everything and looked like he wanted more.

Chapter 11: Feeding Panther Chameleons

Like most other chameleons, panther chameleons primarily feed on invertebrates. However, they occasionally consume small vertebrates and plant material.

The best captive diet for panther chameleons is one that mimics their wild diet, being primarily comprised of a of gut-loaded insects, with occasional fruit or vegetable treats. It is not necessary to feed panther chameleons any vertebrate prey, although some keepers offer the occasional newborn mouse to mature chameleons.

Like most other species, panther chameleons benefit from a varied diet, which helps to minimize the effects of dietary excess and vitamin and mineral deficiencies. However, providing a varied diet is not always sufficient to avoid deficiencies, so it is wise to supplement some of your pet's food with additional vitamins and minerals.

This chameleon is in the process of capturing an insect.

Insects

Insects should form the bulk of the diet for panther chameleons of all sizes. Crickets or roaches make a nice staple, while the other insects can be incorporated to add variety.

Some keepers supplement their captive's diet with wild caught insects, but discretion is advised, as such insects may be contaminated with pesticides or infested with parasites.

The following insects make suitable prey for panther chameleons:

- Crickets
- Roaches
- Mealworms
- Giant mealworms
- Superworms
- Wax worms
- Grasshoppers

Other Invertebrates

Aside from insects, a number of invertebrates make suitable food sources for panther chameleons. However, few are available commercially, so they rarely form more than a trivial portion of a captive chameleon's diet.

A few examples of acceptable invertebrates include:

- Earthworms
- Snails
- Slugs
- Roly polies

Vertebrates

In the wild, panther chameleons occasionally consume small lizards, frogs and birds. While your panther chameleon will remain perfectly healthy without eating any vertebrate prey, it is probably not a problem to offer the occasional pink mouse to your pet. However, too many rodents will quickly cause your chameleon to become obese and suffer from serious health problems.

If you choose to offer rodents to your pet, offer pre-killed, rather than live, individuals, as chameleons lack the jaw strength to kill newborn rodents quickly. Live newborn rodents will not harm your lizard, but it is important to treat all feeder animals with respect, and avoid any unnecessary suffering.

Lizards and frogs should not be offered as prey, as they are likely to be infested with parasites, which they may transmit to your pet.

Prey Size

Mature panther chameleons can easily handle and consume relatively large insects; adult crickets and large roaches are rarely a problem. In the wild, mature adults eat a variety of very large stick insects and similar insects, so they can handle most commercially available feeders.

Juveniles, by contrast, are much too small to consume large insects. In fact, feeding large insects to small chameleons can cause them to become impacted. In some cases, this can be fatal. To avoid such eventualities, offer small chameleons insects that are no longer than the distance between the lizard's eyes.

How to Offer Food

Unless you use a cage with an exceptionally tight mesh, you cannot simply dump a handful of crickets or roaches in your panther chameleon's cage. While your pet may be able to snatch one or two of the insects, the majority will simply crawl out of the cage and into your home.

This leaves keepers with one of two options. You can either offer insects individually by hand or via forceps; or you can use a feeding cup, which will keep the insects contained. Hand feeding is laborious, but acceptable if you do not mind devoting this amount of time to your pet's daily feedings.

If you elect to use a feeding cup, you will need to select a cup that is tall enough to keep the insects contained, and yet short enough that the lizard can reach them via his tongue. Alternatively, if the mouth of the cup is wide enough to accommodate the lizard's body, you can arrange a perch that allows the lizard to get close enough to the insects to reach them.

You can allow insects to sit in the feeding cup for about 24 hours, but do not let them sit in here for any longer. Clean the feeding cup daily with soap and water, and disinfect it periodically.

Feeding Quantity and Frequency

Offer mature chameleons with food every day. Provide your pet with as many insects as he will eat in about 10 minutes. If you wish, you can offer a second meal later that day.

Feed young chameleons as many insects as they will eat in 10 minutes, but provide them with two or three daily meals.

Offering Fruits and Vegetables

Panther chameleons are largely carnivorous, but some individuals will consume leaves or fruit on occasion. While fruits and vegetables are probably not critical for your pet's health, they certainly don't hurt, and many panther chameleons appear to enjoy them. In addition to being rich in vitamins and minerals, most plant material is full of water, which will help keep your chameleon hydrated.

Dark leafy greens are the best vegetables to offer your chameleon. You can simply suspend a leaf in the cage and allow your chameleon to munch on it if he so desires. Be sure to place it near a perch so that your lizard can access it easily. Misting the leaf may catch his attention and stimulate his interest in the food. Remove the leaf after about 24 hours to prevent it from spoiling.

In addition to leafy greens, you can also provide your pet with a number of other fruits and vegetables (see chart). You can leave any leafs uncut, just be sure to attach them securely to the cage or a favorite perch, so the lizard can rip off small pieces. Vegetable-based foods that cannot be used in this fashion should be cut into small pieces or grated, and placed on a plate.

A weekly offering of plant material is likely sufficient for your pet's health (and some individuals may never show interest in plant-based foods), but there is little downside to offering vegetables and fruits more often than this, if he is interested.

Your chameleon may also consume some of the leaves in his enclosure. Interestingly, they often appear to consume fig (*Ficus benjamina*), golden pothos (*Epipremnum aureum*) and other plants that may be slightly toxic. This rarely causes problems for the chameleons, but it is probably wiser to offer vegetation that is known to be safe (such as those listed in the chart), which may usurp your chameleon's desire to munch on his cage plants.

Some keepers worry that panther chameleons primarily consume vegetation when they are dehydrated. Therefore, it is probably wise to evaluate your hydration practices if your chameleon shows interest in vegetation. As long as you are providing water regularly and your chameleon is drinking his fill each time, it is unlikely that his interest in vegetation signals dehydration.

Plant-Based Foods for Panther Chameleons

Here are a few foods that you can offer to your chameleon, which are widely agreed to be safe. Remember that your lizard is an individual, with his own unique preferences and favorites – he may like some and avoid others.

Always wash all fruits and vegetables before offering them to your pet, to help remove any waxes or pesticides.

- Collard greens
- Turnip greens
- Mustard greens
- Dandelions
- Grape leaves
- Hibiscus
- Roses
- Cilantro
- Parsley
- Endive
- Kale
- Broccoli
- Carrots
- Squash
- Zucchini
- Pumpkin
- Kiwi
- Strawberries
- Blueberries
- Blackberries
- Apples
- Pears
- Peaches
- Bananas
- Grapes

Vitamin and Mineral Supplements

Many keepers add commercially produced vitamin and mineral supplements to their chameleon's food on a regular basis. In theory, these supplements help to correct dietary deficiencies and ensure that captive lizards get a balanced diet. In practice, things are not this simple.

While some vitamins and minerals are unlikely to build up to toxic levels, others may very well cause problems if provided in excess. This means that you cannot simply apply supplements to every meal – you must decide upon a sensible supplementation schedule.

Additionally, it can be difficult to ascertain exactly how much of the various vitamins and minerals you will be providing to your lizard, as most such products are sold as fine powders, designed to be sprinkled on feeder insects. This is hardly a precise way to provide the proper dose to your lizard, and the potential for grossly over- or under-estimating the amount of supplement delivered is very real.

Because the age, sex and health of your chameleon all influence the amount of vitamins and minerals your pet requires, and each individual product has a unique composition, it is wise to consult your veterinarian before deciding upon a supplementation schedule. However, most keepers provide vitamin supplementation once each week, and calcium supplementation several times per week.

Chapter 12: Providing Water to Your Panther Chameleon

Like most other animals, panther chameleons require drinking water to remain healthy. However, the relative humidity (the amount of water in the air) is also an important factor in their health. While drinking water helps to keep the lizards hydrated, the moisture in the air helps to keep their skin healthy and prevents respiratory problems from developing.

Providing Drinking Water

Providing ample drinking water is imperative to the health of your panther chameleon. Be sure to provide drinking water at least once each day, but provide your pet with water two or three times each day, if you can. Your lizard may not drink each time you offer him water, but you should still give him the opportunity to drink, should he so desire. This is especially important for young chameleons, whose surface-to-volume ratio causes them to dehydrate rapidly.

Providing drinking water to a panther chameleon requires some ingenuity, as these lizards usually fail to recognize standing water. This means that they rarely learn to drink from a water dish. Instead, panther chameleons prefer to drink droplets of water as they drip down through the vegetation.

Some keepers provide these droplets by misting the chameleon, the perches and plants inside the enclosure. The resulting water droplets will usually entice your chameleon to lap them up greedily. Misting provides the additional benefit of raising the cage humidity, and it tends to wash some surface pollutants from the perches and leaves.

You can mist the cage with a hand-held misting bottle, a pressurized unit or an automated misting system. An inexpensive hand-held misting bottle usually suffices for those caring for a single chameleon, while those maintaining several individuals often find the latter two options more efficient.

Alternatively, drip systems can provide a steady cascade of water droplets, from which your chameleon can drink. Commercial drip systems, which often feature high capacities and adjustable valves, which enable you to alter the drip rate, are available from reptile equipment retailers.

You can also make a simple drip system by poking one or more holes into the bottom of a plastic cup. The more holes you provide, the higher the drip rate will be, so you can adjust the flow rate as necessary by adding or plugging holes in the bottom of the cup.

You want to adjust the drip rate of your drip system to obtain a steady drip-drip-drip cadence. Don't keep the rate so slow that long pauses occur between drops; nor should you allow the water to pour into the enclosure.

Some keepers prefer to give their chameleon dechlorinated or purified or spring water, but others simply offer tap water. Purified bottled water and spring water are typically safe for chameleons, but distilled water should be avoided to prevent causing electrolyte imbalances.

It is wise to have tap water tested to ensure that heavy metals or other pollutants are not present before offering it to your chameleon.

Do not use ice cubes to provide drinking water, despite recommendations to the contrary. While an ice cube will melt and drip into the cage, the resulting water is far too cold for the chameleons to drink comfortably. Additionally, the rate at which the ice melts is rarely sufficient to create a high enough drip rate to attract your chameleon's attention.

Regardless of which method you use to provide water to your chameleon, be sure to provide water at least twice per day for adults and three to four times per day for hatchlings and juveniles.

Removing Excess Water

Providing the drinking water is only one side of the coin – because your chameleon will only drink a small fraction of the water offered, a large amount of excess water constantly enters the cage.

If you mist the cage to provide your chameleon's drinking water, the water will usually coat all of the places in the cage, rather than soaking a single spot. This hastens the rate at which this water can be absorbed by the air, which means that misting rarely causes significant amounts of water to accumulate.

By contrast, drip systems deliver a large quantity of water over a small area. This quickly leads to soaked substrates or even standing water, which is detrimental to your chameleon's health.

If you utilize a very large cage, filled with a number of plants, you may be able to balance the amount of water entering the enclosure with that exiting the enclosure. When this is not possible, you should place a wide, shallow basin below the dripper to collect the water. Discard the water as the container fills, taking a moment to wash it with soap and water before replacing it in the cage.

Contrary to popular thought, adding gravel below a substrate will not enhance drainage. Water resists flowing from a substrate into a different substrate with larger pore size (coarser substrate). Instead, the upper substrate level will saturate completely before it releases any water into the gravel below.

Humidity

Panther chameleons hail from high-humidity habitats, and it is wise to provide them with such in captive settings. In addition to helping them shed their skin more effectively, appropriate humidity is also important for the health of their respiratory system.

The humidity in the panther chameleon's range usually remains above 70 percent for most of the year. Unfortunately, providing such high humidity levels in an open-air habitat is not easy. In practice, you must often settle for humidity levels in the 60 percent range. As long as the chameleon has access to ample drinking water, this does not appear to affect them adversely.

Usually, reptile keepers achieve such humidity levels by restricting the airflow or adding more water to the enclosure. However, because screened cages are essentially necessary for chameleon maintenance, restricting the airflow is not advisable.

The easiest way to increase the enclosure humidity is by increasing the humidity of the entire room. However, constant humidity above 60 percent may not be advisable for your health or the integrity of your home. You must weigh the pros and cons of this method and make the best decision for you and your pet.

Room humidifiers provide an easy solution, but you must be sure to use a high-quality unit, suitable for constant use. Additionally, you must clean the unit regularly to avoid bacterial growth. It is usually preferable to use cool-air units, instead of those that generate steam, rather than water vapor.

If you do not wish to raise the humidity in the entire room, you must add water to the enclosure. The challenge is doing so without causing the cage to become overly wet. Remember, humidity refers to the water in the air, not the water coating surfaces in the habitat.

You will already be adding water to the cage for your animal's drinking needs, as well as for the maintenance of any plants in the enclosure, but you may need to add additional water to keep the humidity suitably high.

Misting is one good way to add additional water to the cage, and because it spreads the water into tiny droplets, misting raises the humidity more quickly than simply pouring water in the cage does. You can also allow some of the water emerging from the drip system to splash into the substrate or the plants' potting soil.

Whichever method you choose to raise the enclosure humidity, be sure to monitor the humidity levels with a quality hygrometer, rather than simply guessing at the humidity level.

Chapter 13: Interacting with Your Panther Chameleon

Chameleons often become stressed by direct keeper-chameleon interaction. Accordingly, it is wise to avoid all unnecessary interactions with your lizard. Doing so will help keep his stress level low and allow him to remain in good health.

If you wish to keep a lizard that can be handled regularly, monitor lizards (*Varanus* spp.) and bearded dragons (*Pogona vitticeps*) make better choices than panther chameleons do. Panther chameleons should be treated as "look but do not touch" pets.

Nevertheless, while you should avoid handling your chameleon as much as is possible, it is occasionally unavoidable. For example, you must remove him from his cage during routine maintenance and you may need to take him to the veterinarian from time to time.

Handling a Panther Chameleon

The very best way to handle your chameleon is to simply move the perch on which your pet is clinging, and avoid directly touching the animal entirely. When this is not possible, the best option is to provide your hand and arm as a perch. Except when medically necessary (such as to administer medication or observe an injury), avoid directly restraining the lizard with your hands.

Generally, you can place your finger (or hand, in the case of large individuals) under the chameleon's chin. Gently apply upward pressure, which will normally cause the lizard to grip your finger (or hand) with his claws. Keep lifting up gently and the lizard will likely crawl right onto you as though you were a tree.

You can simply allow your chameleon to walk around on your hand and arm while you tend to minor duties in the cage. If, however, you need to do any substantial maintenance to the habitat, it is wiser to place him in a temporary holding cage while you carry out the necessary tasks. When it is time to put him back in his enclosure, move him close to a perch and allow him to crawl onto the perch on his own.

Always be patient when transferring a chameleon to or from your hands. Never attempt to pry a chameleon's feet or tail from a perch; instead, be patient and allow the chameleon to move on his own. Sometimes, tickling the chameleon's foot or tail lightly will stimulate them to move more quickly.

Aggressive Chameleons

Chameleons are not typically considered "aggressive" or "dangerous" lizards, but some individuals do respond poorly to their keeper's advances. Most individuals will simply attempt to flee when approached, while others may exhibit darkened colors, gape or hiss at the perceived threat. Some are even willing to bite, should their keeper not heed these warnings.

There is often little that the keeper can do to change the attitude of such pets. Keeping your lizard's stress level low and providing proper husbandry may help. Additionally, you may be able to calm your lizard over time, via repeated, brief and gentle interactions.

In the event of a panther chameleon bite, try to remain calm. Bites from panther chameleons are akin to a strong pinch, and they rarely cause any serious damage (obviously, it is wise to keep your chameleon away from your face as bites here could be more serious).

Usually panther chameleons release their bite fairly quickly. If they do not, it is usually possible to pry their mouth open with a credit card or similar object. A soft plastic spatula is an ideal tool for this task, as the flexible blade is unlikely to injure your pet.

Transporting Your Pet

Although you should strive to avoid any unnecessary travel with your chameleon, circumstances often demand that you do (such as when your lizard becomes ill).

Strive to make the journey as stress-free as possible for your pet. This means protecting him from physical harm, as well as blocking as much stressful stimuli as possible.

The best type of container to use when transporting your chameleon is a plastic storage box or small, screened cage. Add several ventilation holes to plastic containers to provide suitable ventilation.

If the trip is to be brief, the added security, protection and thermal stability of a plastic storage box is generally preferable to the screened container. Conversely, the improved air exchange offered by a screened cage will provide beneficial on long journeys.

Add a few branches or dowels to the container so your chameleon can perch comfortably while traveling. If possible, try to use branches that can be moved directly from the habitat (with the lizard attached) into the transportation container.

Place a few paper towels or some clean newspaper in the bottom of the box to absorb any fluids, should your lizard defecate or discharge urates. You can add a few plant cuttings to the cage to provide cover for your pet, but it is not strictly necessary.

Cover the outside of his transportation cage (do not block the screen, as this would defeat the purpose of a screened cage) or if you are not using an opaque container. This will prevent your pet from seeing the chaos occurring outside his container. Monitor your lizard regularly, but avoid constantly opening the container to take a peak. Checking up on your pet once every half-hour or so is more than sufficient.

Pay special attention to the enclosure temperatures while traveling. Use your digital thermometer to monitor the air temperatures inside the transportation container. Try to keep the temperatures in the mid-70s Fahrenheit (23 to 25 degrees Celsius) so that your pet will remain comfortable. Use the air-conditioning or heater in your vehicle as needed to keep the animal within this range.

Keep your chameleon's transportation container as stable as possible while traveling. Do not jostle your pet unnecessarily and always use a gentle touch when moving the container. Never leave the container unattended.

Because you cannot control the thermal environment, it is not wise to take your lizard with you on public transportation.

Hygiene

Reptiles can carry *Salmonella* spp., *Escherichia coli* and several other zoonotic pathogens. Accordingly, it is imperative that you use good hygiene practices when handling reptiles.

Always wash your hands with soap and warm water each time you touch your pet, his habitat or the tools you use to care for him. Antibacterial soaps are preferred, but standard hand soap will suffice.

In addition to keeping your hands clean, you must also take steps to ensure your environment does not become contaminated with pathogens. In general, this means keeping your lizard and any of the tools and equipment you use to maintain his habitat separated from your belongings.

Establish a safe place for preparing his food, storing equipment and cleaning his habitat. Make sure these places are far from the places in which you prepare your food and personal effects. Never wash cages or tools in kitchens or bathrooms that are used by humans.

Always clean and sterilize any items that become contaminated by the germs from your lizard or his habitat.

Chapter 14: Common Health Concerns

Your chameleon cannot tell you when he is sick; chameleons endure illness stoically. This does not mean that injuries and illnesses do not cause them distress, but without expressive facial features, they do not *look* like they are suffering.

In fact, reptiles typically do not display symptoms until the disease has already reached an advanced state. Accordingly, it is important to treat injuries and illnesses promptly – often with the help of a qualified veterinarian – in order to provide your pet with the best chance of recovery.

Finding a Suitable Veterinarian

Chameleon keepers often find that it is more difficult to find a veterinarian to treat their lizard than it is to find a vet to treat a cat or dog. Relatively few veterinarians treat reptiles, so it is important to find a reptile-oriented vet *before* you need one. There are a number of ways to do this:

- You can search veterinarian databases to find one that is local and treats reptiles.
- You can inquire with your dog or cat vet to see if he or she knows a qualified reptile-oriented veterinarian to whom he or she can refer you.
- You can contact a local reptile-enthusiast group or club. Most such organizations will be familiar with the local veterinarians.
- You can inquire with local nature preserves or zoos. Most will have relationships with veterinarians that treat reptiles and other exotic animals.

Those living in major metropolitan areas may find a vet reasonably close, but rural reptile keepers may have to travel considerable distances to find veterinary assistance.

If you do not have a reptile-oriented veterinarian within driving distance, you can try to find a conventional veterinarian who is willing to consult with a reptile-oriented veterinarian via the phone or internet. These types of "two-for-one" visits may be expensive, as you will have to pay for both the actual visit and the consultation, but they may be your only option.

Reasons to Visit the Veterinarian

While reptiles do not require vaccinations or similar routine treatments, they may require visits to treat illnesses or injuries. However, you needn't travel to the vet every time your chameleon refuses a meal or experiences a bad shed. In fact, unnecessary veterinary visits may prove more harmful than helpful, so it is important to distinguish between those ailments that require care and those that are best treated at home.

When in doubt, contact your veterinarian and solicit his or her advice before packing up your lizard and hauling him in for an office visit. However, any of the following signs or symptoms can indicate serious problems, and each requires veterinary evaluation.

Visit your veterinarian when:

- Anytime your lizard wheezes, exhibits labored breathing or produces a mucus discharge from its nostrils or mouth.
- Your lizard produces soft or watery feces for longer than 48 hours.

- He suffers any significant injury. Common examples include thermal burns, friction damage to the rostral (nose) region or injured feet.
- Reproductive issues occur, such as being unable to deliver eggs. If a lizard appears nervous, agitated or otherwise stressed and unable to expel eggs, see your veterinarian immediately.
- Your lizard fails to feed for an extended period (more than three or four days).
- Your lizard displays any unusual lumps, bumps or lesions.
- Your lizard's intestines prolapse.

Ultimately, you must make all the decisions on behalf of your lizard, so weigh the pros and cons of each veterinary trip carefully and make the best decision you can for your pet. Just be sure that you always strive to act in his best interest.

Common Health Problems

The following are a few of the most common health problems that afflict panther chameleons. Their causes and the suggested course of action are also discussed.

Retained or Poor Sheds

Chameleons do not shed their entire skin at one time, as snakes do. Instead, they tend to shed in numerous pieces, over several hours or days. Occasionally, this can cause them to retain portions of their old skin. While this is not usually a big problem, care must be taken to ensure that the face, tail tip and toes all shed completely. If skin is retained in these places, blood flow can be restricted, eventually causing the death of the associated tissues. Sometimes this leads to the loss of toes or tail tips.

The best way to remove retained sheds is by temporarily increasing the enclosure humidity and misting your animal more frequently. In cases involving small amounts of retained skin, this may be enough to resolve the problem within a few days.

If this does not work, you may need to remove the retained skin manually. If the skin is partially free, you can try to get a grip on the loose part and gently pull the remaining skin free (do not try this if the retained skin attaches near the eyes).

If the retained skin is not peeling up around the edges, you will not be able to grip it. In such cases, use a damp paper towel to gently rub the area in question. With a little bit of water and gentle friction, you can usually dislodge the retained skin.

Always avoid forcing the skin off, as you may injure your pet. If the skin does not come off easily, return him to his cage and try again in 12 to 24 hours. Usually, repeated dampening will loosen the skin sufficiently to be removed.

If repeated treatments do not yield results, consult your veterinarian. He may feel that the retained shed is not causing a problem, and advise you to leave it attached – it should come off with the next shed. Alternatively, it if is causing a problem, the veterinarian can remove it without much risk of harming your pet.

Respiratory Infections
Like humans, lizards can suffer from respiratory infections. Chameleons with respiratory infections exhibit fluid or mucus draining from their nose and/or mouth, may be lethargic and are unlikely to eat. They may also spend

excessive amounts of time basking on or under the heat source, in an effort to induce a "behavioral fever."

Bacteria, or, less frequently, fungi or parasites often cause respiratory infections. In addition, cleaning products, perfumes, pet dander and other particulate matter can irritate a reptile's respiratory tract as well. Some such bacteria and most fungi are ubiquitous, and only become problematic when they overwhelm an animal's immune system. Other bacteria and most viruses are transmitted from one lizard to another.

To reduce the chances of illnesses, keep your lizard separated from other lizards, keep his enclosure exceptionally clean and be sure to provide the best husbandry possible, in terms of temperature, ventilation and humidity. Additionally, avoid stressing your pet by handling him too frequently, or exposing him to chaotic situations.

Veterinary care is almost always required to treat respiratory infections. Your vet will likely take samples of the mucus and have it analyzed to determine the causal agent. The veterinarian will then prescribe medications, if appropriate, such as antibiotics.

It is imperative to carry out the actions prescribed by your veterinarian exactly as stated, and keep your lizard's stress level very low while he is healing. Stress can reduce immune function, so avoid handling him unnecessarily, and consider covering the front of his cage while he recovers.

"Mouth Rot"

Mouth rot – properly called stomatitis – is identified by noting discoloration, discharge or cheesy-looking material in your chameleon's mouth. Mouth rot can be a serious illness, and requires the attention of your veterinarian.

While mouth rot can follow an injury (such as happens when a lizard rubs his snout against the sides of the cage) it can also arise from systemic illness. Your veterinarian will cleanse your lizard's mouth and potentially prescribe an antibiotic.

Your veterinarian may recommend withholding food until the problem is remedied. Always be sure that lizards recovering from mouth rot have immaculately clean habitats, with appropriate temperature, humidity and ventilation, as well as ideal temperatures.

Internal Parasites

In the wild, most chameleons carry some internal parasites. While it may not be possible to keep a reptile completely free of internal parasites, it is important to keep these levels in check.

Consider any wild-caught animals to be parasitized until proven otherwise. While most captive bred chameleons should have relatively few internal parasites, they are not immune to them.

Preventing parasites from building to pathogenic levels requires strict hygiene. Many parasites build up to dangerous levels when lizards are kept in cages that are continuously contaminated from feces.

Most internal parasites that are of importance for lizards are transmitted via the fecal-oral route. This means that eggs (or a similar life stage) of the parasites are released with the feces. If the lizard inadvertently ingests these, the parasites can develop inside his body and cause increased problems.

Parasite eggs are usually microscopic and easily carried by gentle drafts, where they may stick to cage walls or land in the feeding dish. Later, when the chameleon snaps up an insect from the feeding dish, he ingests the eggs as well.

Internal parasites may cause your lizard to vomit, pass loose stools, fail to grow or refuse food entirely. Other parasites may produce no obvious symptoms at all, despite causing considerable damage to your pet's internal organs. This illustrates the importance of routine fecal examinations (which do not necessarily require that you bring your pet into the office).

Your veterinarian will usually examine your pet's feces if he suspects internal parasites. By looking at the type of eggs inside the feces, your veterinarian can prescribe an appropriate medication. Many parasites are easily treated with anti-parasitic medications, but often, these medications must be given several times to eradicate the pathogens completely.

Some parasites may be transmissible to people, so always take proper precautions, including regular hand washing and keeping reptiles and their cages away from kitchens and other areas where foods are prepared.

Examples of common internal parasites include roundworms, tapeworms and amoebas.

External Parasites

Chameleons can theoretically suffer from external parasites, such as ticks and mites, but this appears to be a relatively rare occurrence.

Ticks should be removed manually. Using tweezers grasp the tick as close as possible to the lizard's skin and pull with steady, gentle pressure. Do not place anything over the tick first, such as petroleum jelly, or carry out any other "home remedies," such as burning the tick with a match. Such techniques may cause the tick to inject more saliva (which may contain diseases or bacteria) into the chameleon's body.

Drop the tick in a jar of isopropyl alcohol to kill it. It is a good idea to bring these to your veterinarian for analysis. Do not contact ticks with your bare hands, as many species can transmit disease to humans.

Mites are another matter entirely. While ticks are generally large enough to see easily, mites are about the size of a pepper flake. Whereas tick infestations usually only tally a few individuals, mite infestations may include thousands of individual parasites.

Mites may afflict wild caught lizards, but, as they are not confined to a small cage, such infestations are usually self-limiting. However, in captivity, mite infestations can approach plague proportions.

After a female mite feeds on a lizard, she drops off and finds a safe place (such as a tiny crack in a cage or among the substrate) to deposit her eggs. After the eggs hatch, they travel back to your pet (or to other lizards in your collection) where they feed and perpetuate the lifecycle.

Whereas a few mites may represent little more than an inconvenience to the lizard, a significant infection stresses them considerably, and may even cause death through anemia. This is particularly true for small or young animals. Additionally, mites may transmit disease from one animal to another.

There are a number of different methods for eradicating a mite infestation. In each case, there are two primary steps that must be taken: You must eradicate the lizard's parasites as well as the parasites in the environment (which includes the room in which the cage resides).

Soaking is often a strategy for ridding a lizard of mites, but it is not a viable option for chameleons. In most cases a chemical treatment will be necessary. Consult with your veterinarian, who can recommend a prudent treatment.

You will also need to perform a thorough cage cleaning to eliminate the problem. To do so, you must remove everything from the cage, including water dishes, substrates and cage props. Sterilize all impermeable cage items, and discard the substrate and all porous cage props – including plants and trees. Vacuum the area around the cage and wipe down all of the nearby surfaces with a wet cloth.

It may be necessary to repeat this process several times to eradicate the mites completely. Accordingly, the very best strategy is to avoid contracting mites in the first place. This is why it is important to purchase your chameleon from a reliable breeder or retailer, and keep him quarantined from potential mite vectors.

Long-Term Anorexia

While chameleons may refuse the occasional meal, they should not fast for prolonged periods of time.

The most common reasons that chameleons refuse food are improper temperatures and illness. Parasites and bacterial infections can also cause chameleons to refuse food. Consult your veterinarian anytime that your lizard refuses food for longer than three or four days.

Chapter 15: Breeding Panther Chameleons

Reproduction among captive chameleons has become more common over the last few decades, and panther chameleons are one of the most frequently bred species.

This not only benefits the species, as captive bred offspring help offset the number removed from the wild, but it is also beneficial to chameleon keepers, as captive bred animals make better pets than wild caught specimens do.

Breeding panther chameleons is a relatively straightforward process, and requires only a few basic steps to complete. However, breeding chameleons is not a quick endeavor: The incubation period alone occasionally lasts longer than a year, so prospective breeders must have plenty of patience.

Sexing Panther Chameleons

Obviously, you must have at least one sexual pair of animals to hope for viable eggs and eventual offspring. Fortunately, mature panther chameleons are strongly sexually dimorphic, making it easy to discern their sex. Juveniles, by contrast, lack strong dimorphism, and are more difficult to identify as male or female.

Coloration is the most obvious trait that provides clues to the sex of mature specimens. While females are generally colored in tan, brown, peach and salmon hues, males display bold green, blue, yellow, orange or red colors, depending on their geographic origin and mood.

However, chameleons begin life clad in female-like earth tones, so color only becomes an effective means of sexing panther chameleons once they reach about three to six months of age.

Another important difference between the sexes is size: Males attain much larger sizes than females do. Males usually reach lengths in excess of 15 inches (38 centimeters) in *total* length, while females rarely exceed 13 inches (33 centimeters). However, length alone should never be used as a criterion when comparing animals less than about 12 inches (30 centimeters) in length.

You can also look for the sexual organs of males. The hemipenal bulges of mature male panther chameleons are usually visible at the base of the tail, while females have relatively thin tail bases.

Some experienced keepers are able to distinguish between male and female hatchlings, but discerning the subtle differences between the tails of young panther chameleons is usually difficult for novices.

Males also display more prominent facial crests than females do. This is particularly true of the crests that lie along the snout (called the rostral process). Like color and tail base thickness, these crests are secondary sexual characteristics that develop over time.

Pre-Breeding Conditioning

Breeding reptiles always entails risk, so it is wise to refrain from breeding any animals that are not in excellent health. Breeding is especially stressful for female chameleons, who must withstand potential injuries during mating, and produce numerous, nutrient-rich eggs.

Animals slated for breeding trials must have excellent body weight, but obesity is to be avoided, as it is associated with reproductive problems. Ensure that the lizards are appropriately hydrated, and are free of parasites, infections and injuries.

Cycling

Cycling is the terms used to describe the climactic changes keepers impose upon their animals, which seek to mimic the natural seasonal changes in an animal's natural habitat. For example, keepers may simulate winter conditions by reducing the enclosure temperatures and providing fewer hours of lighting. These changes are often necessary to stimulate captive reptiles into producing eggs, sperm or both.

However, because panther chameleons inhabit areas with relatively consistent annual temperatures and little fluctuation in photoperiod, cycling is not necessary for successful reproduction. Male and female panther chameleons usually exhibit breeding behaviors upon reaching maturity.

While certainly not necessary, some keepers alter the humidity in their chameleon enclosures to mimic the wet-dry cycle experienced by west-coast panther chameleons originating from areas such as Ambilobe, Ambanja or Nosy Be. Specifically, they mist their animals frequently as they are growing and maturing. Then, as the animals near maturity, the keepers reduce the frequency of misting, to simulate a dry season. A few weeks later, they simulate the arrival of the wet season by increasing the amount of misting. A week or so later, they begin breeding trials.

Care must be taken to avoid dehydrating the chameleons while imposing a dry season.

Pairing

Once your panther chameleons have reached maturity (and have been cycled if you plan to do so), it is time to begin introducing the male to the female's enclosure.

Use care when making introductions, as males are sometimes overly aggressive when attempting to mate. Remove the male from his cage (preferably by removing the perch he is standing on), and place it near the female's cage.

Observe her reaction to the male. If she remains calm or does nothing, she is likely receptive and you can move the male closer and allow him to climb onto her perch. If, on the other hand, she begins gaping, rocking back and forth or adopts bold, contrasting colors, she is not receptive, and the male should be returned to his habitat. You can try the process again in a day or two; it may take some time before the female becomes receptive to the male's advances, so be patient. Never place a male with an unreceptive female, as injuries and stress are likely to result.

You can leave the male with the female, but check on them periodically to ensure the pair are not antagonistic toward each other. Try not to disturb the lizards any more than necessary during the process.

Copulation may begin almost immediately, or it may take several hours to occur. The pair may copulate only once, or they may copulate several times over many days. It is usually wise to house the pair together for several days, to allow for multiple copulations, thereby helping to ensure good fertility.

Care of the Gravid Female

With some luck, the female will become gravid (pregnant) shortly after the animals have bred. Gravid panther chameleons tend to adopt darker colors, and they will try to repel approaching males by gaping and displaying bold, pink and black colors.

Remove the male from the female's enclosure once she begins displaying such symptoms. This will help keep her stress level low and allow you to provide better care for her.

Gravid females may alter their behavior in several subtle ways. They may bask for prolonged periods of time or become more reclusive. After initially exhibiting an increased appetite, they typically cease feeding as oviposition (egg deposition) approaches.

Provide females with a suitable egg-deposition chamber as soon as they begin displaying signs that they are gravid. A plastic bucket, pot or storage container makes a suitable chamber. Experienced breeders often transfer females to egg chambers outside of their cages shortly before oviposition occurs, but this only introduces unnecessary complexity to the process that novices are wise to avoid – just place the container inside the female's enclosure and let her find it.

Fill the chamber about two-thirds full with slightly damp soil and pack it gently into place. The soil must not be wet, but it must have enough moisture to allow the lizard to create a stable tunnel and egg chamber. As a rule of thumb, you should be able to compress the soil into a clump when you squeeze it in your hand, without causing any water to trickle out.

Near the end of the gestation, which typically lasts about three to four weeks, females develop very plump abdomens. In some cases, the faint outline of eggs can be seen through the abdominal wall.

Do not handle gravid females unless absolutely necessary, and try to keep their stress level as low as possible. It is often wise to cover the female's enclosure to give her additional privacy.

Egg Deposition

If the female finds the egg chamber satisfactory, she will crawl into the container and dig a small tunnel that ends in an enlarged chamber. She will then turn around and deposit 10 to 40 eggs (usually around 20). After she has completed the process, she will climb back out of the tunnel and cover it completely.

Remove the female after she has filled in the nest, and return her to her enclosure. It is a good idea to mist her thoroughly at this time, so she can rehydrate. Misting her will also help to rinse the dirt off her.

If the female does not find the egg chamber to her liking, she may dig multiple tunnels or simply crawl back out of the egg chamber without depositing her eggs. This can be problematic, as retained eggs represent a very serious health problem.

Try to adjust the substrate in the egg chamber with hopes that she will try again and find your changes helpful. You may need to add water to the substrate or dry out the substrate by mixing in fresh, dry soil. Place her back in the container and leave her alone.

If your female does not deposit the eggs quickly, you must take her to your veterinarian without delay.

Retrieving the Eggs

Once the female has deposited her eggs and you have returned her to her cage, begin excavating the tunnel. Use a gentle touch and take care not to damage the eggs.

Remove the eggs individually and place them in a deli cup or plastic food container, half-filled with slightly dampened vermiculite (most keepers use a 1:1 ratio of vermiculite to water, by weight). When in doubt, subject the vermiculite to the same test used for the egg deposition substrate – it should clump when compressed, but not release any water.

Avoid rotating the eggs while removing and transferring them to the egg chamber. Bury the eggs halfway into the vermiculite and close the container.

Egg Incubation

Panther chameleon eggs can be incubated in a number of different ways. Some keepers elect to place the eggs in a dark closet or cupboard, while others opt to use an incubator, which allows the keeper to set precise incubator temperatures. Either method is acceptable and likely to yield good results.

Keepers seeking to use an incubator can purchase a commercially produced unit or construct their own. Most any incubator designed for use with reptile eggs will suffice, but it is wise to test the unit and ensure it holds consistent temperatures before you are faced with eggs.

You can make your own incubator by filling a 10-gallon aquarium with a few inches of water. Place an aquarium heater in the water, and set the thermostat at the desired temperature. Place a brick in the water and rest the egg chamber on top of the brick. Cover the aquarium with a glass top to keep the heat and moisture contained.

If you allow the temperature of the eggs to fluctuate -- the eggs will be safe as long as temperatures remain between about 65 and 80 degrees Fahrenheit (18 to 27 degrees Celsius) – they may hatch at any time between about 6 and 13 months. Keepers that incubate their eggs in an incubator usually set the temperature between 74 and 78 degrees Fahrenheit (23 to 26 degrees Celsius), and wait similar lengths of time for the eggs to develop. In all cases, individual eggs may progress at different rates, and hatchlings may emerge from the clutch over the course of a month or more.

The reason for the huge discrepancy in incubation times relates to the natural history and ecology of the lizards. Wild panther chameleons typically deposit their eggs during the wet season (if present in their particular location), but they do not hatch until the onset of the following wet season, when prey is abundant. Because panther chameleons may lay multiple clutches throughout the wet season, their eggs must undergo a period of halted development – called diapause – to help synchronize hatching with the onset of the rains. Variation in the length of diapause is responsible for the difference in incubation period between different clutches.

Temperature fluctuations associated with seasonal changes are thought to stimulate the eggs to exit diapause and resume development. However, eggs incubated at constant temperatures eventually resume development on their own.

Some keepers attempt to simulate climactic changes in order to break the diapause period early and accelerate the development of the eggs. A typical temperature regimen for this approach calls for incubating the eggs at about 76 degrees Fahrenheit (24 degrees Celsius) for about three weeks, then dropping the temperatures to about 68 degrees Fahrenheit (20 degrees Celsius) for about eight weeks. Temperatures are then raised back to about 78 degrees Fahrenheit (26 degrees Celsius) until the hatchlings emerge. With this method, the eggs may begin hatching in as little as five months.

Neonatal Husbandry

Once the young begin hatching from their eggs, you can remove them from the egg box and place them in a small cage or "nursery." Do not attempt to remove any hatchlings from their eggs. If any of the young emerge with their yolk sacs still attached, leave them in the egg box until they have absorbed the yolk.

A 20-gallon aquarium with a bare floor and a screened lid makes a satisfactory nursery. Place several small branches in the tank and add plenty of plant clippings to provide the young with some form of cover.

Mist the young several times per day and keep the temperatures at about 80 degrees Fahrenheit (27 degrees Celsius). You can initiate feeding trials within a day or two, but do not be surprised if the young lizards do not begin eating for several days.

Keep the young in the nursery until they begin feeding regularly. At this point, you can begin breaking them into small groups and placing them in screened enclosures.

Chapter 16: Geographic Variations

Panther chameleons – particularly males – from different locations often exhibit considerable variation in color and pattern. The males from each population tend to possess a number of similar traits (the females from most areas look similar).

For example, Nosy Be males often have rather indistinct vertical bars and are often blue or turquoise in color. Conversely, males from nearby Ambanja often display very dark blue or purple vertical bars. Whereas males from both of these locations tend to display blue, green and purple colors when aroused, males from east coast locations, such as Sambava, often display red colors when aroused.

Nevertheless, there is still wide variation among individuals from the same region, and exceptions abound. Some specimens from Ambanja display copious amounts of yellow, while some Nosy Be specimens remain mostly green.

Currently, no subspecies are recognized, and all panther chameleons are classified as the same species: *Furcifer pardalis*. However, this may change as scientists examine the genetic relationships between the various geographic populations.

Whether the species is eventually recognized as a collection of different species or remains classified as it stands, individual animals freely breed with individuals from different geographic origins.

Many panther chameleon breeders pair animals thought to be of the same geographic origin, but this is very difficult to accomplish with certainty. Unscrupulous retailers may label animals with popular locale tags, while their well-intentioned counterparts may simply make mistakes.

The provenance of imported animals is rarely robust, and importers may simply identify animals based on the port city from which they were shipped – despite the fact that the animals in question may have been collected from areas far removed from the port.

The variability of panther chameleons from different geographic ranges, and their willingness to breed with members from different geographic areas only complicates this further. Wise hobbyists do their homework before purchasing panther chameleons, particularly if geographic origin is an important factor.

A few examples of males from different geographic ranges follow, but keep the aforementioned caveats in mind. These are intended to give the reader a general idea of the variation in male panther chameleon color with respect to geography.

Geographic Examples

Nosy Be

Diego Suarez

Ambanja

Ambilobe

Photo Credit: Amwu – Dreamstime.com

Tamatave

133

Chapter 17: Further Reading

Never stop learning more about your new pet's natural history, biology and captive care. This is the only way to ensure that you are providing your new pet with the highest quality of life possible.

Books

Bookstores and online book retailers offer a treasure trove of information that will advance your quest for knowledge. While books represent an additional cost involved in reptile care, you can consider it an investment in your pet's well-being. Your local library may also carry some books about panther chameleons, which you can borrow for no charge.

University libraries are a great place for finding old, obscure or academically oriented books about panther chameleons. You may not be allowed to borrow these books if you are not a student, but you can view and read them at the library.

Herpetology: An Introductory Biology of Amphibians and Reptiles
By Laurie J. Vitt, Janalee P. Caldwell
Top of Form
Bottom of Form
Academic Press, 2013

Understanding Reptile Parasites: A Basic Manual for Herpetoculturists & Veterinarians
By Roger Klingenberg D.V.M.
Advanced Vivarium Systems, 1997

Infectious Diseases and Pathology of Reptiles: Color Atlas and Text
Elliott Jacobson
CRC Press

Designer Reptiles and Amphibians
Richard D. Bartlett, Patricia Bartlett
Barron's Educational Series

Lizards: Windows to the Evolution of Diversity
By Eric R. Pianka, Laurie J. Vit
University of California Press

Essential Care of Chameleons
By Philippe De Vosjoli
i5 Publishing

The Biology of Chameleons
edited by Krystal A. Tolley, Anthony Herrel
Univ of California Press

The Chameleon Handbook
By François Le Berre, Richard D. Bartlett
Barron's Educational Series

Care and Breeding of Panther, Jackson's, Veiled, and Parson's Chameleons
Philippe De Vosjoli, Gary Ferguson
Advanced Vivarium Systems

Chameleons: Care and Breeding of Jackson's, Panther, Veiled, and Parson's
Gary Ferguson, Kenneth Kalisch

Advanced Vivarium Systems

Chameleons: Nature's Hidden Jewels
Petr Nečas
Edition Chimaira

Chameleons: Everything about Selection, Care, Nutrition, Diseases, Breeding.
By Richard D. Bartlett, Patricia Pope Bartlett
Barron's Educational Series

Magazines

Because magazines are typically published monthly or bi-monthly, they occasionally offer more up-to-date information than books do. Magazine articles are obviously not as comprehensive as books typically are, but they still have considerable value.

Reptiles Magazine
www.reptilesmagazine.com/
Covering reptiles commonly kept in captivity.

Practical Reptile Keeping
http://www.practicalreptilekeeping.co.uk/
Practical Reptile Keeping is a popular publication aimed at beginning and advanced hobbies. Topics include the care and maintenance of popular reptiles as well as information on wild reptiles.

Websites

The internet has made it much easier to find information about reptiles than it has ever been. However, you must use discretion when deciding which websites to trust.

While knowledgeable breeders, keepers and academics operate some websites, many who maintain reptile-oriented websites lack the same dedication and scientific rigor.

Anyone with a computer and internet connection can launch a website and say virtually anything they want about chameleons. Accordingly, as with all other research, consider the source of the information before making any husbandry decisions.

The Reptile Report
www.thereptilereport.com/
The Reptile Report is a news-aggregating website that accumulates interesting stories and features about reptiles from around the world.

Kingsnake.com
www.kingsnake.com
After starting as a small website for gray-banded kingsnake enthusiasts, Kingsnake.com has become one of the largest reptile-oriented portals in the hobby. The site features classified advertisements, a breeder directory, message forums and other resources.

The Vivarium and Aquarium News
www.vivariumnews.com/

The online version of the former print publication, The Vivarium and Aquarium News provides in-depth coverage of different reptiles and amphibians in a captive and wild context.

Journals

Journals are the primary place professional scientists turn when they need to learn about chameleons. While they may not make light reading, hobbyists stand to learn a great deal from journals.

Herpetologica

www.hljournals.org/

Published by The Herpetologists' League, Herpetologica, and its companion publication, Herpetological Monographs cover all aspects of reptile and amphibian research.

Journal of Herpetology

www.ssarherps.org/

Produced by the Society for the Study of Reptiles and Amphibians, the Journal of Herpetology is a peer-reviewed publication covering a variety of reptile-related topics.

Copeia

www.asihcopeiaonline.org/

Copeia is published by the American Society of Ichthyologists and Herpetologists. A peer-reviewed journal, Copeia covers all aspects of the biology of reptiles, amphibians and fish.

Nature

www.nature.com/

Although Nature covers all aspects of the natural world, many issues contain information that lizard enthusiasts are sure to find interesting.

Supplies

You can obtain most of what you need to maintain panther chameleons through your local pet store, but online retailers offer another option.

Big Apple Pet Supply
http://www.bigappleherp.com
Big Apple Pet Supply carries most common husbandry equipment, including heating devices, water dishes and substrates.

LLLReptile
http://www.lllreptile.com
LLL Reptile carries a wide variety of husbandry tools, heating devices, lighting products and more.

Doctors Foster and Smith
http://www.drsfostersmith.com
Foster and Smith is a veterinarian-owned retailer that supplies husbandry-related items to pet keepers.

Support Organizations

Sometimes, the best way to learn about panther chameleons is to reach out to other keepers and breeders. Check out these organizations, and search for others in your geographic area.

The National Reptile & Amphibian Advisory Council

http://www.nraac.org/

The National Reptile & Amphibian Advisory Council seeks to educate the hobbyists, legislators and the public about reptile and amphibian related issues.

American Veterinary Medical Association

www.avma.org

The AVMA is a good place for Americans to turn if you are having trouble finding a suitable reptile veterinarian.

The World Veterinary Association

http://www.worldvet.org/

The World Veterinary Association is a good resource for finding suitable reptile veterinarians worldwide.

References

Abigail S. Tucker a, G. J. (2014). Evolution and developmental diversity of tooth regeneration. *Seminars in Cell & Developmental Biology*.

Anderson, S. P. (2003). The Phylogenetic Definition of Reptilia. *Systematic Biology*.

C. J. Raxworthy, M. R. (2002). Chameleon radiation by oceanic dispersal. *Letters to Nature*.

Devi Stuart-Fox, A. M. (2008). Predator-specific camouflage in chameleons. *Biology Letters*.

Djordje Grbic, e. a. (2015). Phylogeography and support vector machine classification of colour variation in panther chameleons. *Molecular Ecology*.

F. ANDREONE 1, F. G. (2005). Life history traits, age profile, and conservation of the panther chameleon, Furcifer pardalis (Cuvier 1829), at Nosy Be, NW Madagascar. *Tropical Zoology*.

F. ANDREONE, F. G. (2005). Life history traits, age profile, and conservation of the panther chameleon, Furcifer pardalis (Cuvier 1829), at Nosy Be, NW Madagascar. *Tropical Zoology*.

Fabian Brau, D. L.-N. (2015). Dynamics of the prey prehension by chameleons through viscous adhesion: A multidisciplinary approach.

Gary W. Ferguson, W. G. (2002). Effects of Artificial Ultraviolet Light Exposure on Reproductive Success of the Female Panther Chameleon (Furcifer pardalis) in Captivity. *Zoo Biology*.

J. CHRISTIAN RANDRIANANTOANDRO, e. a. (2009). POPULATION ASSESSMENTS OF CHAMELEONS FROM TWO MONTANE SITES IN MADAGASCAR. *Herpetological Conservation and Biology*.

Jérémie Teyssier, S. V. (2014). Photonic crystals cause active colour change in chameleons. *NATURE COMMUNICATIONS*.

Michael R. Rochford, e. a. (2013). The Panther Chameleon, Furcifer pardalis (Cuvier 1829) (Chamaeleonidae), Another Introduced Chameleon Species in Florida. *IRCF REPTILES & AMPHIBIANS*.

Rabearivony, J., Brady, L. D., Jenkins, R. K., & Ravoahangimalala, O. R. (2007). Habitat use and abundance of a low-altitude chameleon assemblage in eastern Madagascar. *The Herpetological Journal*.

RICHARD K. B. JENKINS, J. R. (2009). Predation on chameleons in Madagascar: a review. *African Journal of Herpetology*.

Schaeffel, F. O. (1995). A negatively powered lens in the chameleon. *Nature*.

Wever, E. G. (2005). The ear of the chameleon: Chamaeleo senegalensis and Chamaeleo quilensis. *Journal of Experimental Zoology*.

Witte, P.-S. G. (2007). Ultraviolet reflectance in Malagasy chameleons of the genusFurcifer (Squamata: Chamaeleonidae) . *SALAMANDRA*.

Index

Published by IMB Publishing 2016

Copyright and Trademarks: This publication is Copyrighted 2016 by IMB Publishing. All products, publications, software and services mentioned and recommended in this publication are protected by trademarks. In such instance, all trademarks & copyright belong to the respective owners. All rights reserved. No part of this book may be reproduced or transferred in any form or by any means, graphic, electronic, or mechanical, including photocopying, recording, taping, or by any information storage retrieval system, without the written permission of the authors. Pictures used in this book are either royalty free pictures bought from stock-photo websites or have the source mentioned underneath the picture.

Disclaimer and Legal Notice: This product is not legal or medical advice and should not be interpreted in that manner. You need to do your own due-diligence to determine if the content of this product is right for you. The author and the affiliates of this product are not liable for any damages or losses associated with the content in this product. While every attempt has been made to verify the information shared in this publication, neither the author nor the affiliates assume any responsibility for errors, omissions or contrary interpretation of the subject matter herein. Any perceived slights to any specific person(s) or organization(s) are purely unintentional. We have no control over the nature, content and availability of the web sites listed in this book. The inclusion of any web site links does not necessarily imply a recommendation or endorse the views expressed within them. IMB Publishing takes no responsibility for, and will not be liable for, the websites being temporarily unavailable or being removed from the Internet. The accuracy and completeness of information provided herein and opinions stated herein are not guaranteed or warranted to produce any particular results, and the advice and strategies, contained herein may not be suitable for every individual. The author shall not be liable for any loss incurred as a consequence of the use and application, directly or indirectly, of any information presented in this work. This publication is designed to provide information in regards to the subject matter covered. The information included in this book has been compiled to give an overview of the subject s and detail some of the symptoms, treatments etc. that are available to people with this condition. It is not intended to give medical advice. For a firm diagnosis of your condition, and for a treatment plan suitable for you, you should consult your doctor or consultant. The writer of this book and the publisher are not responsible for any damages or negative consequences following any of the treatments or methods highlighted in this book. Website links are for informational purposes and should not be seen as a personal endorsement; the same applies to the products detailed in this book. The reader should also be aware that although the web links included were correct at the time of writing, they may become out of date in the future.

CPSIA information can be obtained
at www.ICGtesting.com
Printed in the USA
BVOW11s0928240517

485051BV00005B/22/P